AGEING: AN ADVENTURE IN LIVING

HUMAN HORIZONS SERIES

AGEING:
AN ADVENTURE
IN LIVING

EDITED BY
SALLY GREENGROSS

A CONDOR BOOK
SOUVENIR PRESS (E & A) LTD

ISBN 0 285 65002 5 casebound
ISBN 0 285 65003 3 paperback

Photoset and printed in Great Britain by
Photobooks (Bristol) Ltd

Contents

Acknowledgements

The Editor is grateful for permission to quote from the following published works:

Old Age by Simone de Beauvoir, translated from the French by P. O'Brian (Andre Deutsch; Weidenfeld & Nicolson, 1972); *A Good Age* by Alex Comfort (Mitchell Beazley, 1977); 'The Educational Experience in Homes and Hospitals' by Sidney Jones, in *Outreach Education and the Elders: Theory and Practice*, edited by F. Glendenning (Beth Johnson Foundation, 1980); 'Encountering Death in Old Age' by David Hobman, in *Social Work Today*, Vol 10 No 2, 5 September, 1978.

Rose Wheeler, author of Chapter 5, wishes to thank Jane Minter and Ken Wright for their helpful comments.

List of Contributors

Sally Greengross
Deputy Director of Age Concern England. This major national body, together with its sister national organisations and some 1,300 independent affiliated local groups, works to provide services and promote the interests of elderly people in the United Kingdom. Sally Greengross writes, lectures and broadcasts frequently on aspects of ageing. Her involvement with the welfare of old people extends internationally, and she works both with Eurolink-Age and as Secretary General of the International Federation of Ageing.

Anne Whitehouse
Journalist and author who was founder editor of Age Concern's quarterly journal, *New Age*. She currently writes for *Community Care* and is a regular contributor to *The Times*.

Dianne Norton
Organiser, researcher and writer specialising in the fields of education and the older adult. She is Co-ordinator of the Forum on the Rights of Elderly People to Education (FREE) and Executive Secretary to the National Committee of the Third Age Trust.

Niall Dickson
Editor of *Nursing Times*, the largest circulation weekly magazine in the world. He trained as a teacher and has

worked for the Centre for Policy on Ageing, Age Concern and Macmillan Journals where he edited *Therapy Weekly*.

Evelyn McEwen
Head of Information of Age Concern England. Formerly a teacher, she has spent many years working as a volunteer with elderly people.

Rose Wheeler
Following her degree in Social Policy, she is currently carrying out research at the University of York into housing and older people. She has published numerous articles on the subject and is a member of Shelter's policy and projects committee.

Li McDerment
Involved in social work and social service training and education for the past 15 years, she works partly in West Berlin, where she teaches Sociology and Social Work at Maryland University, University College Europe, and partly in the United Kingdom, where she is is concerned with staff training and consultancy within the field of residential and day care services.

Ethel Holloway
A Medical Social Worker who worked for some years in the Geriatric Department of University College Hospital, London. Since her retirement, she has co-ordinated the Bereavement Support Group for Age Concern England and Age Concern Wandsworth.

Viveka Nyberg
She has run the Family Welfare Association Bereavement Project in Hammersmith, London, and has conducted courses in loss and change for a number of organisations.

Introduction

By Sally Greengross

Ageing can be an adventure. It offers us new experiences and provides us with the time to enjoy things that may previously not have been possible, due to the heavy demands made on us by our work or by our children.

What we can expect to get out of our own old age, however, will largely depend on what we put into it. Thinking about it, planning in advance and taking hold of the opportunities it gives us for discovery, will provide us with the chance to enhance the later part of our lives.

It is hoped that this book will provide some signposts and guidelines to help older people and those approaching retirement, as they embark on a journey which, while it can be rewarding and fulfilling, is sadly, for some people, seemingly without purpose.

The best adventures are those to which we look forward and which are well thought out beforehand, although it is never too late to start this process. As with many things in life, however, the returns are proportional to what is put in; old age is no exception.

The later stage of life is a time to think about *who* we are rather than *what* our role might be. It is a time to review our past experiences, to reminisce and to seek patterns, order and meaning in our lives. This evaluation not only of what we have or have not achieved, but of what we still wish to accomplish, is an integral part of growing older. The impact of retirement, which for some people can be experienced as a loss of our 'work' identity, may be far less noticeable if we become more keenly aware of our potential and less worried about what we have lost.

Anything we recognise as finite can become more acutely pleasurable, and, as the prospect of available time decreases, the desire to experience life fully and to enjoy all it has to offer may well increase.

Seeing the ageing process as something positive gives us the opportunity to derive great personal fulfilment from the new and different things that may be happening around us. The most fortunate people are those who gain increasing satisfaction as this happens – something that young people may find it hard to understand.

Ageing does not begin when we reach 60 or 70. It is in fact a continuing process, a progression through different stages of life, and it starts when we are very young. Somebody facing retirement today may well have a life expectancy of 20 or even 30 years and in that time can expect to change almost as much as in the first 20 or 30 years of life. Thus, socially defined old age may well turn out to be the final third of our lives and it is time we can use just as creatively as that which has gone before.

Old age is, in any case, almost as much a matter of opinion as a matter of fact. At five years, a child thinks of someone of 20 as old, and we continue to make comparisons like this throughout our lives. Consequently, older people usually think of those who are older than themselves as old and the further from any particular age we are, the more people of that age tend to be placed in a category; this applies as much to young people as to old people.

Our view of ourselves remains essentially the same, however, and we are no different inside because of accumulated birthdays; but other people's attitudes are of critical importance and many of those are very negative about old age and old people. Such prejudiced views, often reinforced by the media, are difficult to overturn. One of the most common misconceptions is that all important human development takes place during the first few years of life and that our capacity to learn new skills, to be creative and to grasp new ideas is greatly reduced with age. This has been shown to be totally untrue. Older people can adapt to new ways of thinking and of living. Today's 80 year-old has, after all, lived through the introduction of such remarkable technical innovations as radio and television and the developments in travel, ranging from steam to the space age, while coping with all the dramatic social changes they have brought with them.

The individuality of older people is important and they do not necessarily comply with expectations. We are all familiar with the images of 'crotchety' old men or 'sweet' old ladies, a view which is as far from reality as if we divided all young or middle-aged people into similar mutually exclusive categories. How much better it would be if everyone accepted older people without stereotyping them. They may be pleasant or unpleasant, good, bad or indifferent, but are as distinct and distinguishable from each other as are people of any other age group.

Life expectancy has increased dramatically during the twentieth century. Progress in public health and medical care has meant that many more people live to enjoy old age, not so much because of an increase in the life span itself, but because they survive infancy. Illnesses and epidemics that were almost invariably fatal in the past are often, in modern industrial societies, virtually unknown or else responsive to treatment, and are increasingly being prevented in developing countries. Few people in this country today expect to die from typhoid, cholera or even whooping cough.

The result of this is that a massive shift in the population is taking place all over the world. Because so many children used to die before they reached adulthood there were always many more young people than old people. What we are now witnessing, however, is the 'greying of the nations'. In 1970 there were 200 million people of 60 or over in the world; by the year 2000 there will be nearly 600 million and by 2025 over 1,100 million. It is striking to think that more than one third of all those people who have reached the age of 65 in the last 2000 years are alive today, and that in the United States of America, a country kept young through constant waves of immigration, in the year 2025 there will be approximately twice as many grandparents as grandchildren. What is particularly important is that, over the next 20 years or so, the proportion of people of over 75 will grow at an even faster rate than before and, although most elderly people remain fit, well and independent (in the United Kingdom only 5 per cent of old people are permanently in any sort of institution), it is amongst very elderly people that we find those most likely to suffer from physical and mental illnesses and who, consequently, need access to a high level of care and appropriate services.

As the proportion of old people grows, that of working people declines. This changing balance in society is of crucial importance in determining how we view our older members and how younger people see their own roles when they are old. As a society, we probably show less veneration for old people than is the case in certain more traditional societies, particularly as the numbers of old people increase and their 'scarcity value' diminishes.

Old people are the guardians of recent history, simply because they have lived through it, so their personal experiences are of immense value in many ways. Many people in these times of increased personal mobility and the breakdown of some traditional family ties, want to retain contact with their roots. Old people hold the key to the immediate family past. A child without grandparents is at risk of losing this sense of continuity. In one generation, let alone two, our way of life has changed almost beyond recognition and direct links with the past are vital. Children in particular are fascinated by stories about what life was like when their grandparents were young, and relationships between grandparents and grandchildren can be very special. Grandparents can give their time and, in particular, time to listen. This is a commodity which is very precious, particularly to the younger generation. However, relationships within families and between the generations are constantly changing and people have to adapt to new circumstances. Anne Whitehouse, in Chapter 1, explores the changing relationships that retirement and older age bring for all of us, and suggests how we might best come to terms with them and enjoy them.

People in general are educated to meet society's perceived needs. We are taught skills in order to make a contribution and, as time is required to pay back the cost of education, it has traditionally been the province of the young. Today this attitude is beginning to change. Learning should certainly not be restricted to the early years; it can provide an opportunity for people of all ages to enjoy new experiences and to broaden their horizons and should be a lifelong activity. Sadly, most retired people do not see it as something relevant to themselves. Education in later life can help to compensate for activities which we have had to give up or which we never had a chance to take up when we were younger. Retired people have ample time to learn and to enjoy new interests.

In the recent past people took it for granted that they would be able to get a job, but now, with ever increasing unemployment and the prospect of fewer people being needed in the workforce in the future, people of all ages are facing the reality of not having paid work, particularly in the form of a full-time job. The whole relationship between work and non-work is beginning to change and we shall all have to reassess the meaning of leisure. Active leisure pursuits, education and many forms of part-time and voluntary activity can provide the key to a fulfilling later life. Older people can make an invaluable contribution as teachers and trainers, sometimes passing on to younger people skills acquired throughout their lives. Learning is not only about sitting in classrooms but about continuing personal development. Older people often experience boredom, loneliness and frustration and the expansion of their horizons could start at any age.

In Chapter 2, Dianne Norton looks at a whole range of leisure and education opportunities for older people and points us in the right directions if we want to benefit from some of them.

To derive maximum benefit from our later years, perhaps the most essential thing is to be in the best possible health. How to look after ourselves and prevent disease, and how best to cope with the disorders, illnesses and disabilities which will undoubtedly affect some of us, are subjects which Niall Dickson investigates in Chapter 3.

For those of us who do stay in full-time employment there is usually a massive change in our life style when we reach the age of compulsory retirement. Most of us face the prospect of lower incomes than we had in the past and many of us are unaware of the range of benefits that is available. Knowing how to find our way through the mass of agencies that may be involved is extremely difficult, particularly for people who do not know what to ask for. The important thing to bear in mind is that people are only claiming benefits which are theirs by right. Many older people have memories of their own youth before the days of the welfare state, when the only help available was handed down in such a way that to accept it was not only an admission of failure but resulted in a loss of dignity. Nearly one million old people in Britain do not take up all the benefits to which they are entitled, sometimes because they are unaware of them and sometimes because of their own inhibitions.

There is no need for anybody to feel grateful, however. Today's old people have lived through two world wars and great deprivation, helping to build the society we all enjoy today. Evelyn McEwen, in Chapter 4, gives us a comprehensive overview of income and benefits, full of helpful information and advice on how to make the best of what we have in later life.

Perhaps the most important asset most of us will ever have, involving, consequently, some of the most far-reaching decisions we will ever make, is our home. Many of us, by the time we reach retirement age, have paid off the mortgage on our own home and there is much to consider and important decisions to be made about whether we want to stay there or move somewhere more suitable. In Chapter 5, Rose Wheeler goes through the whole range of options available to us and offers some very helpful guidance on what we should consider in taking such a fundamental step.

For some people a new life can actually begin in a residential home. The decision, however, to move into residential care is one to be taken only if we are fully informed about what is available and what to take into consideration before choosing a particular type of home. In Chapter 6, Li McDerment looks at various options and indicates the particular features we should watch out for.

For everyone, however, the shock and grief of a death, and the time of bereavement following the loss of a loved one, are the most difficult periods in our lives. Ethel Holloway and Viveka Nyberg take us with great sensitivity through the process of grief and mourning and give us advice about where to go for help, explaining the sort of experiences we can expect during this difficult time. This final chapter will be particularly helpful to people living with and caring for older relatives and friends, as well as to people who themselves suffer bereavement.

Although individually many older people are quite poor,

collectively they control a considerable amount of wealth. The advertising industry understood the potential purchasing power of young people some years ago, and from the 1960s onward directed image-building and campaigning towards them. Having maximised that market, new pastures are eagerly being sought and advertisers are just beginning to understand the importance of the retired section of the population, and are directing attention their way.

Older people do not only have vast potential consumer power, however: they could become a major political force. About 16 per cent of the population is now above retirement age – nearly 10,000,000 people, which means that elderly people make up about a quarter of the voters. The sheer weight of their numbers gives them enormous latent power if they will only take advantage of it. They have a real opportunity to influence social change.

When faced with the prospect of political action, most of us feel there is little we can do, and very few older people are inclined to go out and demonstrate. This is not always what is required, however. The identification of common interests, whether about pensions, social services, housing or any other important issue, and the collective voicing of needs and demands, can achieve dramatic results. Older people can also demonstrate their concern, not only with issues that directly affect their own lives, but also with the future and the kind of society they will leave to the young and to future generations.

No one can deny that ageing brings to the fore a number of problems and difficulties, but it also offers us a great challenge. People whose lives are cut short by an untimely death are denied the opportunity of this adventure and of further personal development. Ageing is an experience worth having.

1 Changing Relationships

By Anne Whitehouse

Growing older can change relationships in many ways, not least because in later life there is more time and less pressure. The bustle of the active years often leaves little time for leisured companionship, whether in marriage or between friends and neighbours. These relationships, however, take on a new meaning after retirement.

Dealings with other people can also change once we are no longer working, because of a change of role. New relationships tend to be more like those we develop on holiday. The 'uniforms' we wear to work have been shed, and some people, finding their new role difficult when it comes to sustaining relationships, become recluses. They see retirement as an opportunity to retire not only from work, but also from other people, and they withdraw and become introverted. Others want and need people and, having relied on their jobs for company, now feel a sense of emptiness in their lives. The ability to relate to others is as important in later life as it was earlier on.

It is not only relationships with friends which change. Family relationships do not stand still. Just as puberty is a period of change, when, during the shift from childhood to adolescence, parents often say their son or daughter is not the same person, so further changes happen when parents see their children shift from adolescence to adulthood and then to total independence.

Parents whose children were once dependent on them now find the roles reversing, as they in turn become dependent on their children. Those who helped a son or daughter set up their first home may themselves need a lot of help, once age has rendered them frail, when arranging their own accommodation. The father who was ever-willing to offer a lift to his daughter may find the roles reversed if he is no longer able to drive.

Age can also bring a mellowing of relationships. Former differences of opinion between parents and children may be reconciled as children themselves become parents and take on similar responsibilities to those once faced by their parents. Some say they feel more like brothers and sisters later in life, and that the generation gap closes. This is especially true when families run into four generations.

Children, too, often grow fonder of their parents as they grow older. They have lost the rebelliousness of youth, and have made their own mark in life. Parents who were once authoritarian are likely to be far less so; instead they respect the achievements of their children and may well be proud of them. A son who has had a period of hostility towards his father may find he becomes much more tolerant when he himself gets a job, marries and has a family. This can be a period of reconciliation between generations. A son can share the experience of being a father with his own father, while the latter develops his new role as a grandparent.

One relationship which tends not to change in old age is that between brothers and sisters. The emotions and ties of infancy and childhood often linger, and may become more pronounced. With siblings, the original childhood relationship often remains unaltered – the 'big sister' or 'little brother role' surviving, even though in adult life two years' difference in age is unimportant.

Katherine was the eldest of five children – three sisters and two brothers – but the death of her own mother when she was ten meant that she took on a maternal role herself. It is a role she has never shed, and it is always to Katherine that the others turn whenever family difficulties arise. Her role is half-acknowledged and half-resented by her younger brothers and sisters who are now themselves pensioners.

There is a lot of talk today about the disappearance of the 'extended family' and the loss this means in terms of the quality of relationships between generations. Popular belief is that families used to be tightly knit, with grandparents, parents and children all living together in an atmosphere of warmth, love and mutual respect.

It is fashionable to blame the young for this change – they have pulled up their roots, more women go out to work, and there has been a dramatic increase in divorce and single-parent families. But it is not always the younger generation who are to blame. Old people often prefer to share a home with people of their own age, and some old people can be difficult to live with and unwilling or unable to adapt.

The nostalgic image of the extended family is, in any case, a myth and greatly overstressed. Probably the generations have always found it difficult to live together, but in Victorian times fewer people lived to old age and, for those who did, the only alternative may have been the workhouse. Now there are more elements of choice about family life styles, with a wider range of housing options and support services available.

Separate households need not mean the end of family ties, and often make for more stable and congenial relationships between adults of different generations by avoiding the awkwardness when two groups of people try to retain some measure of independence in their lives. A lot of sensitivity and patience is required for a multi-generation family to live under one roof.

With advanced communication, there is no reason why

separation by distance should mean families are out of touch. For an older person, family ties become more important as friends are lost touch with or die.

Increasing longevity and more four-generation families means that larger numbers of elderly people may themselves have living parents. The relationship between these two groups may present further challenges in later life. For a couple who have recently retired and whose children have left home, looking after an ageing and frail parent may seem unfair when they are just rediscovering their freedom. The caring years and the years of liberation seem incorrectly balanced – the years without dependents may seem few.

In close family relationships it is often not easy to distinguish who is dependent on whom.

> Nancy never married and lived at home with her parents until the death of her father. She had always talked about setting up in a flat of her own, but when her mother was widowed, she decided to stay with her and give her additional support. When eventually her mother died, Nancy herself was middle-aged and felt unable to start a new life on her own because she had in turn become dependent upon the person who was previously dependent upon her. The plight of such people as they themselves age without the love and dedicated care of a close relative can be especially lonely and sad.

The Role of Grandparenting

The arrival of grandchildren can alter the whole outlook of both parents and grandparents. New parents may feel closer to their own fathers and mothers; grandparents feel a renewal of life, and a chance to pass on their experience and knowledge to a younger generation. They find that they can relive the joy of parenthood without the work it brings.

Grandparents need to be careful not to set themselves up in competition with parents in their relationship with the child. Equally, young parents need to learn how to include grandparents in their children's lives. Some grandparents find they are resented by their children, and accused of 'spoiling' or trying to 'own' the grandchildren. Good grandparenting, however, can help relationships between parents and children, while children generally like the company of their grandparents. They like to hear about the past and this is one way of passing on family traditions.

Relationships across the generations are important for older people, too. Regular contact with close relatives is one of the best therapies for a good long life, and communication with younger people is an excellent way of staying 'young at heart'. Old people who lack contact across the generations may lose interest in and withdraw from the community as a whole, as they lack a forward-looking dimension. The relationship between grandparents and grandchildren re-presents the hope for continuity. It is not uncommon for a sick old person to remain alive until the birth of a grandchild, and to die soon afterwards. It is as if the child is carrying on life for the grandparent, ensuring the continuation of the family. When the death of a marriage partner occurs in old age, the grandchildren are often the ones who give the survivor a new purpose in life. Childless couples sometimes say they feel more deprived by having no grandchildren than no children. Grandparents and grandchildren frequently get on better with each other than with the generation in between, but this does not apply only when children are small. For adolescents who are experiencing a rather turbulent period with their parents, a link with the 'older' generation can often seem less threatening. The same applies to old people themselves, who may be berated by their adult children with comments such as, 'Don't walk without your stick, grandma', or, 'Don't drink too much Guinness, grandad'. The inhibitions which sometimes surround physical closeness between parents and children are often lifted when the link is one generation removed.

The relationship is not always without some tensions, however. Grandparents may be jealous of their grandchildren who, they feel, have a better life than they did. Comments like, 'They are so ungrateful', 'They don't know what it is to go without', are sometimes expressed, and grandchildren may also evoke feelings of guilt and failure in their elders.

There are some grandparents who are not able to fulfil their traditional role. The remarriage of a parent after a death or marital breakdown which results in the in-law taking custody of the children, can deprive grandparents of access to the grandchildren.

Geoffrey and Dora, both in their late sixties, looked after eight-year-old Simon for four years, following the death of their daughter. But when their son-in-law remarried, his new wife took Simon into their home and Geoffrey and Dora saw little of him. The new wife refused to allow them to see Simon any more, or even to let them send him birthday and Christmas presents. Geoffrey and Dora were resigned to waiting anxiously outside the school playground to catch a few minutes with their grandchild.

This kind of situation is not so very uncommon when a partner dies and the surviving partner remarries. The new partner may feel threatened by or resentful of any display of affection between the child and the previous partner's parents, fearing that this will be an obstacle to the childrens' acceptance of the new relationship. This may be even more pronounced after a divorce. When a marriage breaks up, one partner may sever all ties with the other's family in an attempt to forget an unhappy past. Remarriage may bring new grandparents onto the scene, and this may finally break the link.

Cyril and Elisabeth, aged 68 and 74, had not seen their granddaughter Anna for five years since their son, a young captain in the merchant navy, divorced his wife, Jean. Jean had moved in with another man and was terrified that Anna might discover that he was not her real father.

It was to help people in this kind of situation that the law was changed in 1978 (Ref: The Domestic Proceedings & Magistrates Courts Act 1978) to give grandparents the right to apply to see grandchildren through magistrates' courts in cases where parents have separated or where a parent has died. In cases of divorce between parents, grandparents already had the right to apply to the divorce court for a variation of an access order, if this was the only way to see their grandchildren.

People faced with the loss of contact with their grandchildren should make it clear that they want to continue to be actively involved as grandparents. It is important for them, but also for the grandchildren, who may find the grandparents an important link with their own past.

Retirement

What happens to a marriage when a husband and wife find themselves together 24 hours a day, maybe for the first time in their lives?

Work can distract people from other problems and may prevent some couples from facing up to difficulties within their marriage. An uncomfortable weekend ends with the escape to the office on Monday morning; the evening may be spent discussing the day's events and other people's problems, while their own may be side-stepped; the potential row goes into cold storage.

Retirement has been described as a second marriage. However well a husband and wife have got to know each other, it has been in different circumstances. Unfulfilled parts of a marriage can be masked by being busy and going out to work. After retirement they may be impossible to evade.

Work can also be a shock-absorber when things go wrong at home. When this safety valve is removed, the only remaining outlet may be the marriage partner.

Research by the Marriage Guidance Council has shown that many of the problems faced by older couples are connected with changes in life style brought about by retirement. Previously, a couple had a daily routine, and a network of friends and colleagues with whom they were in daily contact. On retirement, all that stable routine may be cut off, leaving couples with only the resources of the marriage.

A recent survey has shown that about eight per cent of people seeking help from Marriage Guidance are in the 60-plus age group. Age Concern has described the lack of counselling and guidance given to older people as a form of 'ageism' or age discrimination. People in the helping professions often consider older people to be incapable of changing their behaviour, ideas and way of life.

Those seeking marriage counselling often have problems which are not dissimilar from younger couples'. They talk in very general terms to start with and say they are not communicating with their partners. The problems often arise from the inability to cope with change. People may say that their partner is no longer the person they fell in love with and married. Then there are particular problems connected with sex, particularly if one partner is more active than the other. This can put a serious strain on the relationship.

Fragile marriages which may hold together while people are working can disintegrate with the added strains of retirement. Too much time in enforced togetherness can be disastrous, especially with compulsory retirement and in circumstances damaging to self-esteem.

A potential danger is that retirement can lead to a tendency to cling to a partner. Problems occur when a couple do not see eye to eye on this. A wife may want to see more of her husband; or she may want more freedom than his presence allows her, especially if she has not worked and is used to having the house to herself. A man may want more of his wife's attention than before; or he may resent her presence as an intrusion.

Derek and Pat's view of marriage was a traditional one. A man's role was to be out at work as the breadwinner; his wife's was to be at home, looking after the children. The arrangement suited them both. Derek enjoyed his work as a proof reader for a large printing firm and the social contact this brought him in terms of staff clubs and sporting activities. Pat was content to focus her interest on the home. When the two children left home, she looked forward to Derek's retirement and the chance to spend more time together.

A few months after retirement, Derek realised how much Pat had grown to depend on him. He appreciated her doting affection, but also felt hemmed in, particularly when he wished to continue to meet former work colleagues on a social basis. He missed the decisions and responsibility of work and Pat resented it when he wanted to get more involved in some of the social activities his firm organised for retired employees.

Derek's concern was that Pat was only interested in the family and home and attributed this to the fact that she had never worked. He felt she had become an appendage to him, not allowing him to live his own independent life as before.

John and Margaret experienced this situation in

reverse. John had worked all his life in a city bank, while his wife, Margaret, after giving up her teaching career to have a family, had enjoyed returning later in life to a part-time clerical job in a hospital. John opted for early retirement and expected Margaret to follow suit, but Margaret was reluctant to lose the satisfaction and sense of responsibility of a job. Her life was a full one which she relished. John expected her to sacrifice that and to centre her life on the home.

When Margaret did stop work it became clear how their respective jobs had concealed differences in their personalities and interests. John was a home-lover, happy in his greenhouse or playing his cassettes. Margaret loved people and missed her work and her colleagues. Margaret felt hemmed in by retirement and thought John was not allowing her enough life of her own. Gradually they learned to capitalise on the interests they both shared and to recognise and accept that Margaret had more to give her marriage if she also had an independent life of her own.

After retirement, home may become the central focus for both partners in a marriage. This is not just a question of sharing the chores but also of striking a balance between shared time and time alone. A good marriage provides companionship that is enhanced by 'doing your own thing' within it. If a woman has regularly gone to a club or class, or wishes to continue her job, her husband should not expect her to give it up just because he is at home. The same applies if a man wants to go on lunching with old colleagues.

People must understand the need to adapt and experiment. Old people often discover a new meaning in their relationship – by finding out what they value most in each other and in their joint life together. They learn what can and cannot be shared, what new interests to develop, and what to discard.

Piles of dirty washing and an unmown lawn will wait when the sun beckons to snatch the moment and go off on a spontaneous day's outing together. Ruts and routine imposed by the working years are best shed after retirement.

Sexual Relationships

Simone de Beauvoir wrote of sexual relations in *Old Age*: 'Not only is the idea shocking, but also comic. The comic theatre is always ready to ridicule the unsuccessful pursuits of the lover who is "past it".'

In a society that claims to be increasingly permissive, the idea of sexual activity in old age remains very much taboo and a subject of mirth. Many old people, vulnerable to the pressures of public opinion, coupled with apprehensions and doubts about their ability to enjoy a sexually satisfying life in later years, may end up conforming to the stereotype that society imposes upon them. As Simone de Beauvoir wrote of the older man, 'He becomes the slave of what other people might say. He inwardly accepts the watchwords of propriety and continence imposed by the community. He is ashamed of his own desires and he denies having them. He refuses to be a lecherous old man in his own eyes, or a shameless old woman. He fights against his sexual drives to the point of thrusting them back into his unconscious mind.'

There are many misconceptions surrounding sex in later life. Among them are: that sex is purely for procreation; that sexual activity is built on physical attractiveness; that sexual drive is highest in youth and declines in middle age; that romantic love is only for the young.

All these factors contribute to poor self-image, which further reduces sexual desire and performance. As a woman grows older, she may start to *feel* frail and ugly, a powerful inhibition to sexual activity. For a man, the equivalent is a decline in physical prowess, performance and achievements by which he has always judged himself.

However, there is no such thing as being 'past it'. Dr Alex Comfort clearly states in *A Good Age*: 'In the absence of two disabilities – actual disease and the belief that "the old" are or should be asexual – sexual requirement and sexual capacity are lifelong.'

Ageing does bring some changes in sexual performance: orgasm is less frequent; more stimulation may be needed to produce an erection; performance may be impaired by illness; but by far the most common cause of sexual non-function is anxiety. Even if intercourse is impaired by infirmity, other sexual needs persist – closeness, sensuality and the need to feel masculine or feminine. And there is evidence to show that to cease sexual activity can be more harmful to health than exertion, as it can lead to severe depression, a further decline in self-image, and can have a distorting effect on the relationship between husband and wife.

It is important to stay active, to continue to take a pride in your appearance and not to be exploited by people who lead you to believe you are over the hill. Boredom, fatigue and worry may greatly inhibit sexual libido. With the pressures of work lifted, many couples discover a new closeness and warmth. Sexual loving does much more than create babies; it brings the feeling of being needed and wanted. Once the need for contraception has ended, sexual relationships can be more relaxed and satisfying.

For those who grew up against the backcloth of a more repressive morality, a strict upbringing may have led to fixed attitudes of what is 'proper' and 'improper'. However, attitudes are changing as society becomes more informed and tolerant. The myth of frigidity and impotence in old age is loosening its hold. People are growing up viewing sex more positively, untrammelled by the folklore expectation of impotence and incapacity in later years. The menopause, far from marking the end of sexual response, often brings a substantial upsurge of sexual enjoyment for its own sake.

As Dr Alex Comfort put it, 'Older people are and always have been sexually active, but now they are getting less embarrassed about it as society gets less uptight about sexuality generally.'

Homosexuality in Old Age
The incidence of homosexuality is generally underestimated, even for young homosexuals who often find that they have to be secretive and not open about their sexual needs. For older homosexuals there is a double prejudice to be faced – their age as well as their homosexuality.

The Campaign for Homosexual Equality (CHE) runs some local groups for elderly homosexuals, while GEMMA runs similar groups for lesbian women, including some specifically for older and disabled people.

Living Alone
Adapting to living alone following a divorce or bereavement can be a more crippling experience for older people, whose lives may have grown so close that when one of them is removed, the other collapses. The feelings of loss are often sustained by older people for a longer period, because they lack the motivation, or even the ability, to reconstruct their lives, and they may well express their emotions less overtly, being inhibited from burdening younger members of the family with their feelings. (See Chapter 7.)

2 Adding Spice to Life: Leisure

By Dianne Norton

It is an interesting semantic coincidence that sage and thyme are often used to flavour our food. In its other sense, 'sage' means 'the wisdom of experience . . . a profoundly wise man (sorry ladies, but that's what the dictionary says) . . . any of the ancients, traditionally reputed wisest of their times'. As for thyme – or time, as the case may be – is it 'on our hands' or 'on our side'? Does it 'hang heavily' or 'fly'? Sage and time are what this chapter is all about. It's about using time happily and productively, and about discovering and rediscovering uses for the sagacity of accumulated wisdom, experience and knowledge which we all possess.

In Britain today the popular image of elderly people does not show them as sages. There is not the tradition of respect that we understand to be common in other cultures. But a revolution is already under way. Older adults are becoming more active and more vociferous in their own cause. They are beginning to earn respect and admiration by a more productive and creative use of their time and talents.

It is only with the last 100 years that retirement has become an accepted phenomenon; the fact that it is a British invention should be a dubious source of pride. Brought in first for civil servants, then policemen, teachers and local government officers, it rapidly spread throughout the civilised world. It required the Registration of Births, Deaths and Marriages Act 1836 to launch the administrative process that would make possible large-scale retirement at a fixed age. The present ages of 60 and 65 were implemented by the 1908

Pensions Act. In the past, people quite simply worked 'until they dropped', but then most of them 'dropped' much earlier. Anyone reaching the age of 60 in the early part of this century might have expected to live another 12 years. Although a man reaching 60 today can, on average, expect to live to be 75, the fact is that the numbers of people surviving today to 80 and beyond are far greater than ever before, and still increasing, and those who do survive are generally fitter and more active than in previous generations. Add to that the present economic climate that has brought 'early retirement' and redundancy in later life to a growing number of people, and we can now envisage a large section of the population who will leave paid employment with up to thirty years of life stretching before them. For some people today their so-called retirement will last longer than their working lives. However you react to that thought, it will be obvious that it puts a very different perspective on 'time'. It is horrifying to think of millions of previously productive and active people 'biding their time' from retirement to death. It is a situation guaranteed to bring death closer. On the other hand, the prospect of those millions of men and women continuing to be productive and active, albeit in different ways, in fact 'making the most of their time', is an exciting one – one that adds a great deal of flavour and zest to the casserole of communal life.

Which brings us to sage . . . Among African tribes, before the introduction of a written language, history was kept and passed on from generation to generation by the wise old men of the tribe. The use of older adults as a resource is a lesson that we in the West are starting to re-learn. One of the most popular forms of educational activity involving older people (as well as youngsters) is based on reminiscence. Exploring the past, particularly as a group activity, has a number of very real benefits. It gets people thinking, keeping their brains active, and it gets people talking, communicating.

Everyone has something to contribute; it offers instant involvement. By discussing and analysing past experience, individuals become aware of a sense of themselves. They can locate themselves in the community, in the patterns of history relevant to their own lives, and they develop important feelings of self-esteem. It is a form of activity that links past and present and very frequently leads on to pursuits of other kinds.

Help the Aged Education Department has developed a tape/slide presentation entitled *Recall*, originally used as therapy for people in geriatric hospitals and residential homes. However, it has proved to be popular and useful in a wide variety of settings. We used to believe that it was morbid or unhealthy for old people to dwell on the past, but now the opposite view is becoming well established.

The Lee Centre is a community centre in the London Borough of Lewisham. It is situated in the heart of a residential area and has been running since 1973. Its doors are always open to anyone from the neighbourhood to come in, to see what's available, attend a wide variety of classes or just to socialise. One of their most successful ventures is the 'Then and Now Club' which grew out of the Retired Group who meet regularly at the Centre. The Then and Now Club discusses current affairs as well as life in the community. Members delve into their personal memories and archives as well as those available at local libraries and record offices to compare their recollections of the past with others. They have produced several booklets of memories and photographs and have been involved in a number of conferences and festivals, including 'Exploring Living Memory' which is rapidly growing into a large and very popular annual event. The 1984 Festival was held at the Royal Festival Hall in London and brought together groups like the Then and Now Club from all over the metropolis.

Another aspect of reminiscence work on display at the 1984

Festival was the translation of memories into drama. There are now several theatre groups which use memories as a basis for their highly entertaining and thought-provoking productions. 'Bedside Manners' started out to entertain old people in hospitals and homes but now also plays to clubs and conferences. They are a small multi-talented company of young people who sing, play and act their way through such topics as a post-war day at the seaside, the history of dance or the story of a musical hall family in the early part of this century. 'Age Exchange Theatre' grew out of work done in schools, where youngsters were introduced to older members of the community in order to learn about their local past. Now such productions as the *Fifty Years Ago Show*, *Alive and Kicking* (a musical romp through pensioners' rights in the style of 'Little Red Riding Hood') and their recently commissioned *Of Whole Heart Cometh Hope*, which commemorates the 100th anniversary of the Co-op Women's Guild, are pleasing a wider audience of mixed ages. Both companies pay careful attention to detail, and the enthusiastic and knowing nods of the audience, their clucks and hums of recognition at a turn of phrase, a detail of dress or a familiar tune, demonstrate the goodness and pleasure to be gained from looking back.

Task Force, now renamed Pensioners' Link, Help the Aged and Community Service Volunteers are all involved in finding ways to exploit, in the healthiest ways possible, the skills, knowledge and experience of older people. Task Force's original approach was to offer the help of school children to cope with domestic problems, such as gardening, decorating and shopping, for old people in the neighbourhood. While this kind of work still goes on, they have now turned their attention more to educational work, with many youngsters becoming involved in pensioners' history groups where the exchange of information is very much two-way, material being used in CSE Social Studies Projects and other kinds of school work. And there is a very important spin-off in this kind of intergenerational work. It is well expressed in the Lewisham Task Force's 1982 annual report:

> Pensioners . . . are the victims of an ageist culture . . . Task Force Policy is to try and confront the problem at its embryonic stage: by becoming involved in schools – infants and secondary; in colleges which train future workers and administrators; and directly by having student placements in our office. By so doing we hope to see a positivist view of the elderly in our society. Old and young sometimes view each other across what seems an almost unbridgeable chasm: by bringing the two together in mutually beneficial circumstances, we hope to activate the changes.

This is an aspect of education that will be referred to again. Suffice it to say at this point that the education of all ages of the general public is desperately needed, in order to create the climate of opinion in which older people are readily welcomed into a whole range of educational establishments and in which they themselves feel comfortable and eager to involve themselves in that kind of activity.

'The Creative Craft Project' was set up by the Help the Aged Education Department in order to provide opportunities for older people to pass on their skills to youngsters in schools. Later they were involved in a nationwide competition called 'Side by Side'. Contestants devised projects involving traditional cookery and a wide variety of craft skills, local history, illustrated biographies and nature walks. It is hoped that much of the work done for the competition will become a regular feature of school life.

In Bristol the CSV has launched several projects which give retired people the opportunity of using their skills and their time in a satisfying and productive way. 'Friends of Gingerbread' are senior and retired volunteers who can offer assistance to one-parent families. The idea of three-generational links is beginning to spread and CSV is offering short training courses to acquaint the volunteers with the problems of single-parenting.

'RSVP' (Retired Senior Volunteers Project) also places older people in local school offices where they help with the work involved in running local community associations, PTA groups, social and sporting clubs and other similar neighbourhood activities. At one school a retired engineer and enthusiastic gardener now has 19 pupils learning about horticulture under his guidance. In the same areas the 'Sesame' projects aim to bring together mature volunteers with young people trying to set up their own businesses. In all these activities, just as in the less formally organised case of the retired sailor from Jersey who regularly comes into his local comprehensive to help the children with their oral French lessons, older people are using their time productively, involving themselves in interesting and worthwhile activities; and, while they are learning something about the younger generation, the youngsters are definitely learning a lot about them and about what it is like to be old . . . valuable lessons that will improve their outlook and attitudes and prepare them for their own later years.

This field of sharing experience and knowledge involves different kinds of agencies. As we have seen, it is happening in schools and community centres, through voluntary agencies such as Pensioners Link, Community Service Volunteers and Help the Aged. Many other voluntary bodies, both nationally and on a local level, offer opportunities of this kind. Many areas have a Volunteer Centre which should be able to give details of opportunities for older people. Otherwise the local Citizens' Advice Bureau or Age Concern may be able to make helpful suggestions.

Being a volunteer means a lot more today than it did in the past. There are still important and interesting jobs to be done in offering services to those less mobile individuals who have always needed help; but there is also a whole host of possibilities for the more specific employment of skills and experience. If the idea of becoming involved, for instance in local school activities, appeals, individuals should take the initiative and go along to the school and offer their services.

In some areas of the country the use of volunteers is well developed. The field of adult education is one that has suffered badly through financial limitations of late, but also it is an area where organisations such as the Workers' Educational Association and National Adult Schools have for several generations actively involved 'lay people' in educational programmes. It is true but unfortunate that in some contexts tensions, amounting even to hostility, can arise between volunteers and professionals, mainly when the latter feel that their jobs or 'clients' may be threatened by 'amateur' activity. However, we are entering a period of new awareness. A new role for the professional educator is beginning to be accepted. In the years to come there will be an increase in the numbers of volunteers involved in educational programmes, and there is a definite need for a new breed of professional who will guide and support the volunteer effort. Dr Eric Midwinter compares this new kind of educator with the teacher who welcomes parental participation in the school, as opposed to the one who sees such 'participation' as unwelcome interference. The adult education tutor will become an enabler. He or she will develop the skills needed to 'make things happen' with the assistance of volunteers. In this way, educational opportunities should become more widely available.

Some examples of this kind of activity are already evident. In Cambridgeshire, where community education was pioneered, the Local Education Authority involves many volunteers in the management and operation of the education system. Some work as tutors in the County's Special Learning

Programmes, offering basic literacy and numeracy to adults. Of course, the 'Adult Literacy Scheme' is an excellent example of a highly successful project that involves volunteers all over the country. In Cambridgeshire, volunteers are running 'senior citizens' groups', providing transport for elderly students, involving themselves with administration at the swimming pools, fund raising, helping in crèches and canteens, as well as tutoring and acting as counsellors. About a quarter of all the volunteers are retired. Sensibly, the Community Education Service supplies some training to its volunteers, although it is agreed that more is generally needed.

In Southampton, volunteers, with the help of a community worker, have set up a day centre for Asian elders, and the 'Outreach Project' has brought educational activities to elderly people in sheltered housing schemes. The project is managed by a committee including representatives of various interested agencies, volunteers and the elderly residents themselves.

In the world of adult education, 'Attleborough' has become quite well known. This Norfolk town was the scene for a televised experiment which became known as the Attleborough Experiment. Promoted by the Local Education Authority, the first step in the experiment was OWL (On With Living) Day . . . where local groups and individuals were invited to demonstrate their skills so that anyone interested could 'See it: Try it: Do it', as the publicity said. The eventual outcome was a whole spectrum of courses, from car maintenance to 'O' level English, readily available in the community and all taught by volunteer tutors. The LEA supports and administers the scheme and covers the expenses involved . . . an excellent example of voluntary and statutory co-operation. Apart from the benefit derived by the students, the volunteer tutors claim that for them pleasure was in 'the enjoyment of sharing skills and enthusiasms with others, and the satisfaction of observing the pleasure that the class was giving the students'.

These are just a few examples of schemes that offer older adults a chance to share their skills and wisdom with others. Many other organisations provide such opportunities: the Workers' Educational Association, Women's Institutes and Townswomen's Guilds, Society of Friends, many local churches, pensioners', local conservation and historical societies and trades union bodies. C. Fernau, in an article in *Labour Education*, puts forward the interesting suggestion that people should be trained, while still at work and approaching retirement, in the skills necessary for them to make valuable voluntary contributions to the life of their community in later life. For the older adult, free of the restraints of paid employment, the gift of talent and wisdom will be amply rewarded by the pleasures of involvement, the stimulus of the challenge, the acquisition of new knowledge and the general sense of physical and emotional well-being that such activity brings.

'The University of the Third Age' is the fastest growing movement involving older adults in educational activities. According to the French, who coined the phrase, the first age is that of childhood and development, the second is your active working life, the third is active retirement, while the fourth age represents senility and dependence. The theory goes that if you are active and stimulated enough in your third age the fourth age can be put off or avoided all together. In France and now over much of the continent, universities of the third age are actually attached to universities, where committees of retired people negotiate for the use of facilities and expertise. But in Britain, U3A has developed as a self-help or mutual-aid organisation and is as suitable for a small market town as for a larger centre with more educational facilities. It is interesting that in Cambridge, where the first U3A was launched in 1982 and where it is enormously successful, with over 700 members, it has no official connection with the university at all. U3A London, with an equally large membership, is based in the university itself.

A national charity has now been set up called the Third Age Trust. Its role will be to service already existing U3As and to promote the development of new groups. It publishes a newspaper which is circulated to members throughout the country and employs two part-time organisers to visit areas where new initiatives may fruitfully be helped into existence. Many of the already active third age groups are located in medium size towns such as Yeovil, Saffron Walden and Harpenden, and grouped together in emerging networks in the West Midlands, South Devon and West Yorkshire. They are run entirely by committees of members who are not only students but teachers as well. One of the original objects of the movement states that the aim is 'to create an agency where there is no distinction between those who teach and those who learn, where as much as possible of the activity is voluntary, freely given by members of the University to their fellows.' In reality, although not everyone wants or feels able to teach, members are thoroughly involved in organising social, cultural and recreational activities, coping with the administrative work involved, fund raising, producing newsletters, and so on.

Research is another undertaking which third age groups enjoy. Some are involved in specific research projects connected to whatever course of study they may be pursuing. This style of investigative education is an exciting and attractive one. It helps to get people away from the idea that education remains as they knew it in their childhood – that is, classroom based. It encourages individuals to use and develop new talents and mental faculties in getting out and discovering things for themselves. The second kind of research advocated by the Third Age Trust is that which is stated in another of the original objects: 'To undertake investigation into the process of ageing in society, and especially into the condition of the elderly in Britain and the means of improvement.' Britain lags dramatically behind the rest of the world in research of this kind. In America, three or four times as much is done to investigate the processes of ageing and the potentials of older people. By involving themselves in such projects, third age members are fulfilling what they see as their responsibility to their peer group and to society at large, to educate and '. . . assail the dogma of intellectual decline and make those in their later years aware of their intellectual, cultural and aesthetic potentialities . . . to educate British society at large in the facts of its present age constitution and of its permanent situation in respect of ageing.'

The U3A style is also designed to be accessible to everyone. Study groups can meet in people's homes, and there are already two or three instances of this happening where the group leaders or tutors are in fact disabled and might otherwise not be able to participate. They are also offering activities to people on a one to one basis. In a pilot scheme in Edinburgh, a retired couple are visiting a number of housebound people in order to guide their progress in creative writing. Future prospects might well include the extension of U3A activities into hospitals and residential homes for older people.

There is no limit on what subjects U3A groups can pursue. Some are involved in highly academic studies, but on other days of the week they might well be attending or tutoring a course in home electrics or craft work. Every group decides its own programmes on the basis of what the members want and what they are prepared to offer. It is the first national movement that seeks to co-ordinate and develop new outlets for the skills, knowledge and experience of older people. Members are committed to educating, in the broadest sense of the word, themselves, each other and the general public.

Many older people watch a lot of television. The U3A movement wants to encourage its members to use 'the box' in a more positive and creative way. It is a point that will, hopefully, be adopted by other providers of educational activities, too, such as LEAs working in residential and sheltered homes. There is a great wealth of excellent material on television, from dramatised novels to first rate documentaries. Most of the TV companies now make freely available very good and stimulating back-up material for those who want to pursue, in greater depth, topics covered on the screen. Small groups can be formed to discuss whatever they have been watching and plan ways to find out more, or they may simply want to look at popular programmes in a more critical fashion. If 'Dilemmas in Dallas' get people exercising their brains and communication skills, then three cheers for the Ewings. It has been said that no one learns anything from television, but it is in fact the beginning of the acquisition of much knowledge. TV is surely just the thin end of the wedge of new technology that will, in the foreseeable future, open up our leisure lives. It has already been demonstrated that many older people are interested in computers and that computers offer the kind of home-based activities so beneficial to people with many kinds of disabilities. Older adults must not be left behind in the technological revolution. This is another area where all available resources must be ferreted out and tapped. But providers may have to learn from their elders that they are ready, willing and able to take advantage of all these new learning possibilities.

Educational Gerontology is relatively new to this country although fairly well developed in America. Wisely, interested Britons are determined to tailor-make their own brand of this discipline and not simply to accept the American version as unquestioningly as we have the hamburger. We have, however, accepted as a guide the definition of Educational

Gerontology coined by the American, D. A. Peterson. Included are three components:

(1) educational endeavour for middle-aged and older people; (2) public education about ageing which will improve general attitudes towards older people; (3) pre-service and in-service education of professionals and practitioners for working in the field.

1981 is already regarded as an historic landmark in the field of education and elderly people. Prior to that time, some projects were being developed in various parts of the country but little was known of what was going on generally. One or two meetings and conferences had been devoted to the subject and a limited amount of literature had been produced on the topic. Then, in January 1981, a number of interested parties came together to form the 'Forum on the Rights of Elderly People to Education' (FREE) to act as an information network and a pressure group. Partly as a result and partly because of the swelling tide of realisation that around 10 million people were now 'retired', with few challenges and opportunities for a fulfilling lifestyle, the subject of education and elderly people began to be recognised as a growth area. Things began to happen, and things that had been happening in isolation for some time began to be noticed.

Since 1981 the number of organisations, both statutory and voluntary, concerning themselves with education for elderly people, has noticeably increased. The subject has been on the agenda of many national conferences and a considerable number of meetings and conferences have been convened to deal specifically with the issues. The number of publications, books and articles devoted to the topic may not yet fill a single bookshelf, but a significant increase is obvious. However, this burgeoning of activity, discussion and writing does need to be underpinned with serious and systematic thought to ensure that the present momentum is directed in the most beneficial way. A conference convened at the University of Keele at Easter 1984 and code-named EGG – the 'Educational Gerontology Group' – has set itself the task of looking at the theoretical background and the implications for practical action. It is also much concerned that research should be increased and co-ordinated and that findings should be disseminated to the best effect.

Perhaps the single most important point to arise out of that initial meeting is this: while most practitioners, such as nurses, social workers, etc., working with elderly people will receive some training using a geriatric model of old age – that is, one that assumes some degree of malfunctioning to be normal – very few, if any, will be introduced to a gerontological model, or one that looks at the old person as a basically healthy, normal person. The result is that almost everyone going out into the community and taking a professional interest in elderly clients will be approaching them with the inbred attitude that they are to some degree less than normal. On reflection, this is an appalling state of affairs. Is it any wonder that the general public harbours so many myths about the capabilities of the old? One of the aims of EGG is that, in the future, university departments and colleges who deal with the training of professionals, will make available, as part of their standard educational package, elements that inculcate a realistic picture of ageing. Even professionals who may only be peripherally involved with older adults, such as architects, lawyers, bankers, merchandisers and certainly adult educators, should confront these issues during their education.

One of the myths rife in this country is that all old people are the same. How absurd. Hopefully, the kind of activity described earlier, where youngsters are meeting and working with their elders, will do much to make them realise that old people are unique and interesting individuals. Just because they have reached a certain age, they have not suddenly become one face in an amorphous mass. To some degree, the media fosters this view when it gives well-meaning and enthusiastic publicity to elderly people who do seemingly extraordinary things. There was a case recently of a lady in her 90s who attended a 'Return to Learning' course at Middlesex Polytechnic. She spent so much time being interviewed by the papers and appearing on TV that she barely had time to attend the lectures for which she had come! On the one hand, this kind of exposure does tell people what is possible in later life, but it can also have the effect of saying that this individual is exceptional and has done something that 'ordinary' people cannot do.

The most common myth of all is, of course, the one about old dogs. Maybe you cannot teach an old dog new tricks, but we do know that old people can go on learning. Everyone has some kind of learning experience every day. Every time you go somewhere you have never been before, you are learning a new route. You do not have to sit down in a classroom, behind a desk, in order to learn. The tools we have used to measure 'IQ' are mostly designed to work on children and they can only quantify a narrow range of mental functions. It has now been established that these tools are not suitable for assessing the ways in which adults' minds work. We also know that 'intelligence' means so much more than that nebulous figure that is obtained by such tests. A person's whole experience, the time and environment into which he or she was born, combined with talents, capacities, native wit – whatever you care to call it – affect the cerebral capabilities.

Another difficulty in trying to discover people's capacities through the use of tests is that it is now well established that older people in poor health perform less well. In other words, much of what might be seen as mental impairment is caused by physical maladies. Felicity Huppert, a psychologist, in a paper presented in Oxford in 1981, says that in tests, elderly subjects suffering from hypertension, and also many postmenopausal women with 'low vital capacity', showed 'a marked deterioration in memory while the performance of elderly subjects with normal blood pressure remained stable'. She concludes: 'The idea that mental deterioration in the elderly may be secondary to adverse physiological changes has important implications: ageing is an irreversible process but some of the physiological changes which accompany ageing may be reversible. By treating the physiological conditions (hypertension, low vital capacity, etc.) it may be possible to halt or reverse the accompanying mental deterioration.'

Another British psychologist, Dr Sidney Jones, has specialised in monitoring the effect of educational activity on elderly, frail people in residential homes and geriatric hospitals. In *Outreach Education and the Elders: Theory and Practice*, he records a dramatic result.

One of the six patients attending an art class at a West London geriatric hospital is Mrs H, aged 83. When the class began, meeting twice a week, Mrs H was completely chairbound as she suffered from severe arthritis and had previously had a slight stroke. The medical staff reported at the time that she was indifferent to her surroundings, had difficulty in propelling her wheelchair, and was frequently incontinent. A mental test yielded a score of only 5 out of 10, and showed, for example, that she knew neither the name of the hospital nor of the Queen.

Three months after the class started the medical staff made the following report:

Marked physical improvement. Where previously needed two nurses to propel her wheelchair, now wheels about unaided. She is still chairbound but now only requires minimal help with dressing and feeding, and is much more co-operative with staff. Washes herself, cleaner in her habits, completely continent. Brighter mentally. Most dramatic improvement, noticed by all staff and her daughter who says she is brighter and easier to talk to. Mental test score 7 out of 10.

Dr Jones goes on to explain the chain reaction that this exercise has triggered off. The work in the group stimulates conversation. The staff take an interest and realise that Mrs H is more than just an anonymous charge. This gives them something to talk about with her and she looks forward to the next class. She takes greater care in getting herself ready, and the more interested she becomes, the more she improves her powers of concentration. She is exercising her eyes, hands, memory, her powers of communication and vocabulary. If these results can be achieved with the very old and frail, just think what can be done for those still active. And such success stories have benefits in other directions, too.

To quote Felicity Huppert again:

There is little doubt that negative attitudes towards ageing and the belief that mental deterioration is normal, have contributed to mental decline in the elderly. The development of positive social attitudes based on the awareness of growing numbers of old people that their mental capability remains high beyond retirement, is certain to exert a beneficial effect on maintaining or improving mental functions. If this is accompanied by the early detection and prevention of cardio-respiratory changes which commonly underlie mental deterioration, we can anticipate a reduced incidence of mental deterioration among the elderly in the future. Improved mental function will mean less reliance on the social and health care services and the expectation of a better quality of life for a large section of the population.

There is obviously a close connection between a healthy body and an active mind. Each generation that reaches retirement has grown up through an age of improved nutrition and better health care. More and more older adults are seeking ways to stay or even become physically active. Octogenarian marathon runners are becoming positively common. The general improvement of leisure facilities in the community means that greater numbers of older people have access to sport and recreation.

Swimming has always been regarded as just about the best exercise for maintaining all-round fitness. Some local baths now offer special sessions for pensioners, recognising that they may not want to join in with the hurly-burly of younger water babies or that they may feel a little self-conscious about appearing in public in a swimming costume if they have not done so for several years. If special sessions and classes are not available, then people should ask for them. After all, these facilities are there to offer a service to the community.

Leisure centres in various parts of the country are opening their doors to retired people and welcoming them in for a whole day's activities. They may try out various sports, take part in lectures and discussions, have a reasonably priced lunch and perhaps end the day at a sociable tea dance. In Huddersfield, Mrs Edith Bently, a retired nurse, approached the local centre and, with the full co-operation of the staff, launched 'OWL Day' (Over 50s Wednesday Leisure Day). In only a few weeks, with publicity in the local paper, several hundred people were enjoying the day. This is another good example of a volunteer supplying the impetus and working hand in hand with the providers.

In Lewisham, the '50 Plus Club' got started with help from the Local Authority and the Sports Council; while some of the group do go swimming together, most of their activities take place in a centre normally used for children and include darts, cards, bingo, snooker, keep-fit and yoga. The important thing is that the group is organised by its members. They decide what they want to do and expect individuals to volunteer to organise specific activities. There does appear to be a very real trend in this direction. Whether it is the academic classes of some branches of the U3A or the complete mixture that you find in others, or the purely recreational offerings of the 50 Plus Club, older people are 'doing it themselves' and seeking out ways of making better use of community facilities and their own energy and talents.

Health education is another important field of development. The 'Tooting Action for Pensioners' (TAP) in south London have made close contact with their local hospital and its department of geriatric medicine. They find themselves involved in consultations and conferences and they have a representative on their Community Health Council who is specifically there to put the pensioner's point of view. A general feeling of concern among the group members that they were not getting the kind of treatment they needed from their GPs, led to an approach to the WEA who supplied tutors for a 12-week health course. They covered, not just practical topics such as 'the chest', 'the bladder', acupuncture and diet, but also important, if sensitive, subjects such as the right to die. Every session ended with a programme of exercises.

In America, monitoring of programmes where senior citizens were taught about the intricacies of health care, proved that those involved made much more efficient use of the resources available. Not only did this lead to an improvement in their general health and well-being but also to savings within the system. The kind of work that TAP is doing aims at teaching older people to help themselves. The recently launched 'College of Health' also offers individuals the resources to take better care of their own health. Working in conjunction with Help the Aged and the National

Extension College, they have produced a course entitled 'Fit for Life' which aims to answer the need of elderly people for information, inspiration and reassurance about health problems.

The development in this field demonstrates the eclectic style of education so appropriate to later life. Information of a highly practical nature is being passed on; discussion and analysis of important issues is encouraged; programmes of activities are designed to enhance involvement, to make the most of the resources of the individual and to stimulate physical and mental activity; and, finally, individuals and groups are making intelligent demands on the system and learning to appreciate what impact they can have on changing things to their own advantage.

Many older people fail to realise that the education system as a whole should be seen as a service to the community: a service on which they could and should make demands. Too often their definition of education is closely tied to their own experience – and for many that means a short and unsatisfactory spell at school. It is centred on learning the basic skills of reading, writing and arithmetic and is very different from the expansive concepts of modern education. The images that spring to mind often discourage them from re-entering the education scene.

Even for those who can get over this psychological hurdle, there are other barriers which deter them from taking up adult education. First, there is the cost. Most Local Education Authorities give concessions to people on pensions. A very few offer free non-vocational classes and, in London, the ILEA allows pensioners to attend as many classes as they like for only £1. Most give half-fees, but because in some areas adult education classes are very expensive, even a half-fee can amount to as much as £21. Some LEAs only give the concessionary fees if you actually go and ask for them and seem to do little to advertise that they are available. The overall picture, then, is one of unfair, unequal fees. Retired people thinking about moving to another area, and keen on adult education, might do well to think carefully about which LEA gives the best deal.

The range of classes on offer also varies dramatically. The general Bill of Fare at adult education institutions, especially in the day time – which is, after all, when most retired people prefer to participate in activities outside the home – is not very mouth-watering. The majority of classes seem to be in the subjects which someone, somewhere, has decided are what old people want or ought to learn – that is, crafts, cookery and gentle keep fit. However, many adult educators are open to suggestions and would be only too pleased to try and provide a more palatable diet if they were made to see that the demand is there.

Classes certainly do not have to take place in schools. Many adult education organisers are now very involved in providing tutors wherever groups of older people meet, such as at luncheon clubs, in sheltered housing schemes (where classes may, and should, be open to other elderly people who live locally), and in day centres. They are beginning to see the need to take education out into the community. Hopefully, older people are also beginning to realise that they can ask for this service to be made available to them.

Libraries are also beginning to broaden dramatically their field of operation. In some areas they see themselves as a multi-faceted service to the community, providing information, entertainment and education as well as making available books, records, video cassettes and much more. Many libraries have available equipment that would be useful to older readers with disabilities. In Leicester, the Library Service has started library clubs which meet in local libraries on the one afternoon a week that the buildings are closed to the general public. Old people are brought in, sometimes with the help of the community police. Age Concern workers help with the organisation, provide tea and advice on a range of practical problems. The librarians are there to discuss books and a programme of films, talks, discussions and quizzes is laid on. In their latest exemplary initiative, Leicester has created two 'bookmobiles' with wheelchair hoists that will take such club activities, along with books, puzzles, cassettes, etc., around the country to homes and day centres, so that many more older people can benefit from the service.

This kind of activity, and the others discussed in this chapter, are successful because they start from a careful consideration of the needs of older adults. Physical needs such as sufficient toilets, not too many stairs, comfortable seating, adequate and frequent transport . . . providers need to take a close look at their facilities and see if they are suitable. There are emotional needs as well. Almost all educational and leisure activities have a strong social element. The getting out, the making contact, the possibility of meaningful communication – are all vitally important. And older people have intellectual needs, too. They need to find ways to go on using their brains and their skills. They need to find ways of focusing on themselves in their present situation. How often are retired people referred to as ex-taxi drivers, retired bank managers or whatever. In other words, we label people according to what they were and not what they are. Is it surprising that so many old people truly believe that they are 'has-beens'?

Older people have to begin to believe that they are important individuals, that they each have something to contribute. What is needed is a concerted effort by all generations to rid our society of the dangerous myths about later life. Retirement can be a creative and productive time, but older people themselves must start to generate the impetus that will lead to a satisfying life style. Individuals have to learn how to make the most of the resources available in the community, and that includes the resources within themselves. It is difficult to describe the wide variety of activities, as has been done in this chapter, without making it all sound positive. The harsh truth, however, is that most of these activities are one-offs. There are library clubs in Leicester and a Retirement in Action centre in Sunderland. In Lewisham you can attend the Then and Now Club and in about 30 towns you can become involved in your local U3A. But there is still an enormous educational wasteland between these fertile herb gardens. Hopefully, these examples of good practice will some day be replicated in other areas, but in today's economic climate it is doubtful if we will ever reach a state where wide and good facilities are *provided* for the majority of the millions of people no longer in paid employment. That is why the way forward must be through the mobilisation of all our resources, including the individual human resources of Britain's elderly community. The wisdom, experience, skill and sagacity are there and the time is ripe.

3 Health in Later Years

By Niall Dickson

Human mortality, and the fear of death that often goes with it, have led people of many differing cultures to seek ways of extending the lifespan. The universal biological mechanism, known as ageing, has often been regarded as a threatening process, or at least one that should be slowed down if at all possible. Thus far Nature has had her way. The ambition to be young again must remain unfulfilled. Physical ageing is still both inevitable and irreversible. Yet old age is not an illness; if it were, we would not be able to discuss health in old age since it would be a contradiction in terms. Ageing can lead to dysfunction, but its effects are usually not serious, it is not a common cause of death, and it is only loosely connected with chronological age.

There are a number of complex theories which seek to explain the ageing process, although it is accepted that we begin to age after an initial life phase of growth. The rate at which our bodies grow old varies between races, genders and individuals, and why some people grow older more slowly than others remains a mystery. As in many other areas, there are experts who believe it is predominantly a matter of genes (nature) while others point to variables in the environment (nurture). It is clear that both play a part in the ageing process.

There are, then, a number of physical changes that occur after we reach maturity, which could be termed as ageing, and towards the end of life these accumulate and we begin to use the term old age. In our society the physical characteristics common in older people have become less important in identifying them as a group – instead we have tended to use the end of working life or the start of pension entitlement as the gateway to 'old age'. We talk about 'pensioners' and 'old people' as if they were synonymous. In this way, the gradual ageing process has been distorted to look as if people become old overnight and as if this radical change means that they withdraw from the mainstream of society. Being an old man, in this context, is more about how he is regarded than what he is – more about society's attitudes than his physical state.

The ways in which different cultures view their older members vary considerably; even within the western world there are differences. Historically, old people have held all kinds of positions, ranging from the Bakhtiari tribesmen of Persia, where the old men were left to die when they could no longer cross the river, to gerontocracies, which are societies ruled by older people. Old age has not always been chronological, tied to the years after the age of 65. Societies in which most people died at around 30 or 35 had a completely different perspective, as no doubt have those African cultures today in which people are said to live until they are 120 or 130. Now that we can expect to live to between 70 and 80 years, our attitudes are changing, too. This is perhaps one reason why people in their 60s rebel against the description 'old'. With 20 or 25 active years ahead of them, why should they accept such a depressing tag?

All this supports the 'I am as young as I feel' attitude. With its disregard for chronological age, it is as good a starting principle as any for healthy living in later life.

Nevertheless, it is important to be aware of the physical and mental changes brought about by ageing, as many of them can be ameliorated or compensated for, while others are irrelevant and should be disregarded, such as baldness or the greying of the hair.

Bones become less dense with age and therefore break more easily. This also causes the spine to contract, resulting in some loss of height. Water loss from the discs in the back has the same effect.

We lose muscle and brain cells as we grow older. There is a tendency, therefore, for some strength to disappear, but this can be minimised by exercise which increases the power of the remaining muscles. To lose brain cells sounds even more alarming, but as the process begins from the time that we stop growing, it is not nearly as drastic as might first appear. The most apparent effect on older people is loss of short-term memory, although neurological change can also damage the sense of balance. The belief that people lose intelligence as they grow older depends entirely on how you define intelligence – if experience is included or regarded as central, then it could be said to increase with age. The image of the sage or wise old man is evidence that such a view was taken in earlier times.

Although the senses are affected by age, the change is often not noticeable. This does, however, make it all the more important to look after the eyes and ears, and have them regularly tested.

Sex hormones decline with age, and of course female fertility ends with the menopause. The male sex hormone diminishes throughout adult life. Neither of these changes need mean reduced sexual activity, however, and certainly should not be regarded as a reason for abstinence.

Other body-regulating mechanisms, such as those controlling body temperature, blood pressure and the bladder, can be impaired with age, but again the effects are often insignificant, and where they are not it is almost always possible to do something about them. It would be foolish indeed to deny age-related changes, but they should not be regarded as the essence of growing older. For most people they are peripheral and should not be a bar to health and fitness.

Offering advice to old people about keeping healthy is, in a way, the height of impertinence. What distinguishes them from everyone else is their survival; if anything, the advice should come from them. Of course, longevity and health are not the same, although it has to be conceded that no one has yet found a way of maintaining health after death!

Although poor health is by no means an inevitable part of old age, it is true that the older a person gets the more likely he is to become ill. The important point here is that many diseases can be prevented or cured or their symptoms controlled.

A positive attitude is essential, not only because it is usually the realistic one, but also because a resigned approach invites defeat. No one really knows how far our minds control our bodies, but the traditional medical model, which sees patients as a set of components which either break down or become worn out, is now being increasingly challenged by doctors and other health professionals. In fact, it has long been recognised that it is possible to 'die of a broken heart', or simply 'to give up'. If the mind can play such a decisive role in a negative fashion, there is every reason to suppose that it can also promote health.

If we are prepared to concede that the body is not simply an 'island of cells', it follows that its 'fitness' will be determined as much by external factors as by the wearing down or malfunction of its internal workings on their own. To accept this is to acknowledge that our health is to a much greater extent within our own control than has been recognised in the past. It also involves seeing health not merely as freedom from disease, but as a positive state to be promoted and defended whenever possible. Sadly, health is like peace: it is only when war breaks out that we become aware of what we have lost.

This wider view of health incorporates the social and physical environment, relationships, financial position and so on. Throughout our lives these factors change in varying degrees and in later life they can be the subject of major traumas. For example, many experience some loss of income on retirement, and breaking off from the world of work may also result in the end of long-lasting friendships. Children grow up and away, new neighbours move in and friends die. All these *can* cause older people to withdraw from the world with potential harm to their health.

It is clear that most older people do not withdraw, and there is evidence, in this country at least, that they are relatively well integrated. Nevertheless the danger is there, and maintaining social contacts should be regarded as an essential contribution to positive health. The physical environment in which an elderly person lives becomes more crucial with advancing age. The young person is sensitive to cold temperatures and can in any event usually adjust, using an automatic mechanism in the brain. This causes him to shiver which cuts off the blood supply to the skin and thereby reduces heat loss. Elderly people, on the other hand, are less sensitive and disease can impair the body's 'thermostat', exposing them to the increased risk of hypothermia (loss of body temperature). The chance of falling victim to hypothermia can be reduced by keeping active, if that is possible, and by being sensible in the use of heat and insulation in the home. Thermometers in the sitting room and bedroom are useful and inexpensive monitors, and it is always worthwhile investigating the various forms of financial assistance to help with heating costs.

Common sense will also dictate that physical hazards around the home are removed. The frayed carpet, stiff door, or loose pot handle may have been manageable, if undesirable, in a younger person's home, but they become much more dangerous if the occupant is frail or even just a bit slower on his feet. Good lighting, non-slippery floors and secure rails are other safety essentials.

A Healthy Diet

The links between diet and health have long been recognised, although it is only comparatively recently that strong evidence has come forward to associate certain types of food with many western diseases. The all too common high fat, sugar, salt and low fibre diet is now being mentioned in connection with heart disease, strokes and even certain types of cancer. A sudden and radical switch is probably not advisable at any time, but, in later life especially, a gradual change towards more healthy eating is the best approach.

The ground rules are relatively simple and are no different for elderly people than for the rest of the community. Old people do not necessarily need to eat less (or more, for that matter) than anyone else. Their intake should be related to their level of activity. If for any reason the body is doing less work, then they will need to consume less food. For example, a man who has been used to heavy manual occupation will probably have to reduce his food intake on retirement to avoid obesity, although he would also be well advised to take up some form of exercise. The foods to be particularly careful with are those with plenty of carbohydrates, like cakes, biscuits, jams and tinned fruit and the fatty foods such as oils, dairy products and fat on meat. Both sugar and fat are held to be contributory factors in heart disease, as well as prime causes of obesity.

As any doctor will confirm, we do not need a chart or even scales to tell us that we are overweight. An honest look in the mirror and a gentle squeeze of the hand around the midriff provides as accurate a picture as any. To be overweight is unhealthy at any age and for older people it is even more dangerous since they are already more prone to disease.

Under-eating is equally a threat to health and is a real problem for many people who live alone and find it difficult to motivate themselves to cook a proper and balanced meal. Women, who have for years slaved over a stove for their spouses and families, find that they simply cannot be bothered when their husbands have died and the children have left home. Although this attitude may be a symptom of something else, like depression, it should be resisted. The incentive to eat properly can be restored by cooking for someone else once more, and so a good idea might be to invite a friend round to share a meal.

On the other hand, if a physical dysfunction is preventing an old person from cooking, help should be sought from the occupational therapy service who can assess the difficulty and advise on aids or adaptations to remedy it.

There are probably enough dietary and food publications to cover half the landmass of this planet, and therefore it is unnecessary here to go into great detail about what constitutes a good diet. However, here are some basic guidelines.

1 Protein is the body-building catalyst and is essential – eg., fish, eggs, beans, bread, cereals, etc.
2 Fibre is now regarded as being equally important – bran, wholemeal bread, etc.
3 Alcohol – this should only be taken in moderation; it does provide energy but also harms the liver.
4 Salt – avoid it altogether as an additive if at all possible; there is probably enough in prepared foods anyway.
5 Dairy products – fine for energy and minerals but should be kept in moderation because of their fat content.
6 Fat – avoid it.
7 Fresh fruit and vegetables – regarded as good in every way.

In short, less fat, less sugar and more fibre.

Keeping Fit

Exercise is important at any age and is possible even for the most frail and disabled individual. The first hurdle is, again, attitude of mind. The traditional idea that the last phase of life should be devoted to 'putting one's feet up' is now thoroughly discredited. Exercise helps to keep arthritic joints free from pain and lack of it increases the chance of heart disease.

Clearly, the choice of exercise and the extent to which it strains the body must depend on the individual's physical state. No one who wants to avoid a premature grave should embark on a 20-mile jog without a proper build-up and training. Nor need all exercise be of the strenuous variety – walking and simple movements to music are both commendable forms of exercise which may be appropriate. Anyone with a disability or illness should consult their doctor before participating in sport or exercise. The guiding rule should be that if it can be moved it can be exercised.

Attitudes towards the involvement of elderly people in sport have changed, and even those who have not participated for many years will find many openings and often a useful social outlet as well. Other forms of exercise, such as swimming, gardening and odd jobs around the house, are also beneficial, and it is possible to take additional exercise simply by altering daily habits. Try walking to the shops or using a bicycle for visiting friends.

Anyone in doubt about the most suitable exercise should talk to their general practitioner. Those who are unused to physical exertion are always advised to take things step by step and not overdo it.

There are literally hundreds of books and magazines on keeping fit, and most contain sound advice – the only caution is that they may be aimed at younger and fitter people. Remember that it is important that the programme is geared to the state of the individual. Keep-fit classes are becoming very popular and usually there are sessions especially for older people. The same guidance here applies about contacting the doctor beforehand and letting the instructor know any disability or condition that might affect your health. Exercise is for everyone and even people who are bedridden should be helped to use as many parts of their body as they can. It is also an activity that need not be monopolised by the young – indeed in later life it may be more important in maintaining health and vigour.

Regular Check-Ups

Having looked at how the body can be maintained, let us now concentrate on what might be termed 'regular servicing'. After the age of 40 or thereabouts, it is probably advisable to pay an annual visit to the doctor and it becomes more important the older one gets. Illness is more prevalent in elderly people and, in the event of a serious illness, early detection is almost always desirable. The check-up may include the taking of blood pressure, urine sample and chest examination.

Dental decay is the most common disease of them all, and an old person whose teeth have survived until late in life probably does not need advice on how to look after them. Having defended them from the ravages of modern food, these people are in a good position to point younger people onto the right road. Older people, however, sometimes do start to neglect their teeth and this is usually a sign of some kind of emotional or depressed state.

Good teeth or properly fitting dentures are vital for proper articulation, adequate diet and morale. Everyone's teeth should be examined by a dentist at least twice a year and whenever they cause discomfort or pain. The National Health Service provides two check-ups and elderly people on supplementary benefit are entitled to free treatment thereafter. Everyone else has to pay for any treatment required following the check-up, although, depending on income level, some help may be available. The dentist will be able to provide the necessary forms.

People who have dentures need not go to the dentist so frequently – once every two years is usually sufficient. Visits are still required because our mouths change shape over the years, whereas dentures obviously do not, and adjustment or replacement may be required. Ill-fitting dentures are like bad teeth; they can cause discomfort and embarrassment, as well as affecting eating habits and speech. Oral hygiene is still important, even after we have lost our own teeth. As well as following guidance from the dentist about looking after dentures, it is a good idea to clean the mouth out daily with either toothpaste or a mouthwash.

Regular check-ups for the eyes, at least once every two years, are worthwhile, even if there is no apparent loss of, or change in, vision. Some diseases are not immediately apparent and early detection is a great advantage. Under the National Health Service, everyone is entitled to at least one free examination a year, and any subsequent consultation on clinical grounds is also free. Spectacles are free for those on supplementary benefit.

There is a natural loss of flexibility in the eye as part of ageing, and this can make glasses necessary to cope with close-up work. In most people this becomes apparent in middle age, and by their 60s little further degeneration occurs. If there is any sudden loss of vision, pain in the eye or blurring, a doctor should be consulted immediately.

There are two common eye conditions that can appear in old age, although neither of them need lead to blindness. Cataract, that is the clouding over of the lens, is the best known and can be treated either by the prescription of glasses or, if necessary, by a simple operation to remove the lens and replace it with a plastic one. The operation can be performed under local anaesthetic. Glaucoma is the next most common, and is caused by the blocking up of the tubes that carry fluid from the eye. This causes a build-up of pressure on the eye ball, and, as with cataracts, it can cause complete loss of vision if it is not seen to. It can be successfully treated by pills and eye drops or, if necessary, again with a simple operation. A lot of elderly people are unnecessarily frightened by the prospect of going blind – the chances of this happening are small and it is wise to keep this in mind if some deterioration in sight does occur. Most people with reduced vision derive enormous benefit from talking books and other reading aid facilities, such as special lights and magnifying glasses. Information about these and other services can be obtained from the Royal National Institute for the Blind.

Our hearing starts to deteriorate from our 30s onwards, although for most of us the loss is imperceptible until we reach about 60. Even then the deterioration may be so slight that we can adjust without the need for medical intervention. However, it is vital to seek help if there is any substantial defect in hearing. Sometimes there is a reluctance to admit to a hearing problem, partly because it is taken as a sign of ageing and also because, in the past, deafness was mistakenly associated with stupidity. Prejudice against deaf people persists, but there is a much greater understanding than even a few years ago. Some shops now carry a sign which indicates that their staff are trained to be sympathetic and understanding to people with a hearing loss.

Admitting that there is a hearing problem is therefore the first step towards doing something about it. All that may be required is for the ears to be syringed regularly to remove wax. Alternatively the GP can refer his patient to an ear, nose and throat specialist who may prescribe a hearing aid or suggest surgery.

Hearing aids are becoming increasingly sophisticated and discreet, and after a period of adjustment should become quite easy to handle. No one should buy a private aid without having first tried one on the National Heath Service and having had independent professional advice. There are also various aids for the home, such as amplified doorbells and telephones with either a light or a built-in amplifier.

Lipreading can be a great asset, and the reader should not hesitate to ask people to face them when talking. There are lipreading classes and support groups, details of which can be obtained from the British Deaf Association, or the Association for the Hard of Hearing.

To be cut off from the world of sound can be a lonely and frightening experience and nowadays is often unnecessary. Although hearing loss is the most common characteristic of old age, its effects are for the most part very limited, and, where they do make themselves felt, much can be done to reduce them.

Our feet require special attention in later life, if only because the chances are that they have been ignored and badly treated since birth. This neglect can result in immobility and that in turn can lead to isolation and depression. Old people do tend to have problems with their feet; but here again they can be minimised with regular care and proper professional help, if required.

Correctly fitting shoes and socks or stockings will help, and careful attention should be paid to washing the feet daily and drying them gently but thoroughly. Nails should not be kept long and should be cut across the top, and not down the sides. If you have any pain or corns, cuts or ulcers, the doctor or chiropodist should be consulted as soon as possible. Anyone who suffers from poor circulation, in particular those with diabetes, should be receiving regular professional attention, and the GP should be consulted if the feet become white, dark, red or purple as this may indicate a circulatory problem.

Chiropodists will treat many conditions of the feet and it is worth persevering to obtain their services. There is a shortage of properly trained practitioners and in particular the National Health Service has huge waiting lists for non-emergency treatment. Caution is required in this area as it is possible for anyone to put up a plaque outside his door (often with a string of near-meaningless letters after his name) and open for business as a chiropodist. The important letters to look for are SRCh (State Registered Chiropodist) – if a so-called chiropodist does not have these it is better to look elsewhere. Anyone wishing to check whether a chiropodist is on the State Register and entitled to those letters can do so by writing to the Registrar of the Council for the Professions Supplementary to Medicine, York House, Westminster Bridge Road, London SE1.

Unsteadiness

As we grow older we are more likely to fall over. Man is the only mammal to move around in an entirely upright position and he spends the first couple of years of life struggling to achieve and maintain it. One consequence of ageing is the impairment of the self-correcting mechanism in the brain which allows us to walk around with such a high centre of gravity. If this is the cause of unsteadiness, the risk of falling can still be reduced by using a walking stick or frame and by ensuring that hazards around the home are removed.

Unsteadiness can also result from drugs (especially those which lower blood pressure) and the cause of any fall should be fully investigated and not considered as a part of growing old. It is also quite common for elderly people simply to trip, as the muscles are less strong and their joints may be a little stiffer. Obviously, well fitting shoes, not slippers, and attention to flooring around the house, will help to reduce the chances of this kind of fall. For people who have a history of falling, it is sensible to devise routes around the house and then try to stick to them. For example, the easiest way from a chair in the sitting room to the kitchen should be worked out and remembered, which will also help those whose sight is not good. A variety of walking sticks is available and rails and other adaptations can be fitted to create a safer and more secure environment for an unsteady walker. Any health professional should be able to direct an elderly person to the source of help in this area, although contact is usually through the Occupational Therapy Department. Some elderly people who live alone arrange for a neighbour to call every day to check that they are all right, and there are mechanical alarms on the market which can give reassurance. These usually have one drawback or another, but can provide comfort and security.

The psychological effect of falling should not be underestimated. Some elderly people lose faith in their ability to get out and about after a fall, and need much reassurance and confidence building. The key point to remember is that in many instances the cause can be isolated and treated, and even when this is not the case, there are sophisticated devices to provide support.

Incontinence

Of all the conditions associated with old age, few are more emotive or myth-ridden than incontinence. It is still not a topic for polite company, and among all the supposed pitfalls of growing old it must rank among the most feared. Incontinence is unpleasant and embarrassing. There is no getting away from that, but it is not confined to elderly people and babies and, more importantly, the vast majority of incontinence sufferers can be successfully treated. It is therefore quite wrong to regard incontinence as a natural by-product of the ageing process, about which nothing can be done except to pretend that it does not exist. It is vital to seek professional help and establish the cause, as this will determine what action can be taken.

A common reason for incontinence, but one that is all too often overlooked, is medication. Bedwetting during the night, for example, can often be attributed to sleeping pills and diuretics. The drugs given to control high blood pressure actually increase the rate at which urine is formed, so they, too, can precipitate incontinence.

Another rather obvious cause is frailty – if whenever we wanted to go to the bathroom we had to wait for someone to help us, how many of us would remain continent? Many elderly people who are slow on their feet face too long an interval between the urge to go and reaching the toilet. As with drugs this can usually be minimised. One way is to set a regular time to go, thereby anticipating the urge; the journey can also be made easier and certainly the bathroom should be adapted for anyone who is infirm or disabled. There are very simple but effective devices such as secure handrails and raised toilet seats, and these can transform what would otherwise be a very frightening and insecure environment. Again, the occupational therapist will be able to advise on this and there are now quite a few aid centres around the country where the range of products can be viewed.

Infection and illness of various kinds do lead to temporary, or in some cases, permanent, incontinence – stroke victims, apart from mobility problems, can lose control of the muscles at the neck of the bladder and anyone who is confused (often a temporary state) can be incontinent.

Women who have borne children can suffer from so-called 'stress' incontinence resulting from impairment of the muscles during childbirth, while in men the prostate gland can expand to such an extent that it blocks the natural flow and inhibits control.

Even when an operation is not appropriate, or other forms of treatment cannot restore continence, the unpleasant effects can be minimised. Incontinence pads are much more sophisticated nowadays and they should leave the wearer dry while absorbing urine. The 'Kylie' sheet performs the same function in the bed. Some experts now estimate that 80 per cent of those suffering from incontinence could be successfully treated.

Strokes

Strokes are yet another condition wrongly associated exclusively with being elderly, although they are more common among the middle-aged than the old. A stroke or cerebrovascular accident (CVA) is a blockage in the brain which deprives a part of it of its blood supply and therefore kills off the brain cells. Strokes can be fatal, but for the many who survive there may be some loss of speech or movement, often on one side of the body. Strokes are associated with high blood pressure and narrowing of the arteries.

The onset is usually sudden and there is often a loss of consciousness, difficulty with breathing, as well as confusion and problems with speech and sound. After the attack, some of the lost faculties may return, though some permanent paralysis or speech impairment is common after a major stroke.

The psychological impact is enormous; some stroke victims undergo a personality change that can be very distressing for their friends and relatives. This will be exacerbated if speech is lost. They also experience great frustration at their inability to perform simple tasks like dressing. Depression is very common as the stroke victim seeks to adjust to his new situation.

Immediately following a stroke, an elderly person may appear severely incapacitated, although many make a good recovery. Nursing care is critical. Bedsores, muscle stiffness and permanent damage to joints may be avoidable and the physiotherapist, speech therapist and occupational therapist will be heavily involved in the rehabilitation process.

Heart Failure

There are three main causes of heart failure: high blood pressure, disease in the heart valves and narrowing of the coronary arteries. Coronary heart disease can first appear as 'angina' which may first present itself as a brief but severe period of chest pains. However, with the correct medication, diet and exercise, people with heart disease can live to very old age without such an attack.

The old chestnuts of weight, tobacco and stress are the enemies once again, and medical advice is likely to be to lose weight, stop smoking and avoid tension.

Cancer

Cancer is without question the most feared disease in the developed world. It is fairly common, unexplained and, surprisingly, diagnosis is still widely regarded as a death sentence. Today many forms of cancer can be treated and in some a complete cure is available if the disease is discovered in time. Cancer tends to be more malignant in the young. For some elderly people life expectancy may not even be affected by the cancer diagnosis.

Treatments vary depending on the type and extent of the disease. Drugs, radiotherapy and surgery are the most conventional forms of treatment, although some success has been claimed for alternative approaches, involving diet and changed life styles.

On the darker side, there are still cancers for which no cures or effective treatments are available, and in such cases the relief of pain is the top priority. There are now specially trained staff to care for cancer patients and, in a growing number of areas, units or hospices for the terminally ill have been established. The emphasis, even in these places, is on home care whenever this is possible.

Mental Health

Mental problems are yet another area where fear reigns supreme. 'I wouldn't want to get like her,' is a common response to an elderly person who appears muddled about the world around her. There remains widespread misunderstanding about the fundamental differences between mental handicap (a state which exists at birth, for which there is no treatment and which relates to low intelligence) and mental illness which can occur at any age and intrinsically has nothing whatever to do with intelligence. Until comparatively recent times the mentally handicapped and the mentally ill shared society's contempt and embarrassment. The separation of the two groups in institutions in the twentieth century represented an attempt to remove from both the 'mad' label which had in turn replaced that of witches and evil-doers.

Mental illness, like physical illness, always has one or more causes – sometimes it is not possible to discover what they are, but that does not mean they do not exist. Our mental health, like our physical health, can be affected by environmental as well as physiological changes.

It is hardly surprising that mental problems are rather more common among older people, especially those who have to adjust to traumatic events. When a spouse dies, a family moves away, a job is given up or a physical function is impaired, the natural reaction is one of depression. If, however, all these events come together, or occur within a relatively short period of time, this natural response can get out of hand and little or no adjustment is eventually made. This is obviously the point at which to seek fresh help – if the cause of the depression is not clear, then the GP should be consulted straight away.

The first task in treating such conditions is to work out what is the cause and, if that cannot be dealt with or its effects minimised, anti-depressant drugs may sometimes be prescribed. General practitioners may put elderly people in touch with the psychiatric services if they feel that their specialist training and orientation is required to identify or manage the presenting conditions. This can involve a visit from or to a consultant psychiatrist (there are now some who specialise in the mental health of older people), support from the community psychiatrist nursing service or attending a day hospital. Being referred to psychiatric specialists often causes great alarm, especially when the patient is not confused and does not necessarily feel ill at all. The stigma of being thought of as 'mad' has not disappeared and a great deal of reassurance is required. There is no shame in being seen by a psychiatrist and it certainly does not mean that the individual is 'mad'. Contrary to popular belief, there is nothing odd, magic or frightening about what the psychiatric services do. Most treatment involves nothing more than talking.

For many people, one of the greatest fears is of becoming confused and incoherent. Anyone who is suddenly affected in this way should be referred to a doctor. The main reasons for a rapid deterioration in mental functions include strokes and heart conditions (which influence blood supply to the brain). However confusion may result from drugs, or the combination of drugs being taken or, in some cases, even constipation can be a contributing factor. Depression, which may or may not have a physical cause, can lead old people to be disorientated in one way or another. Whatever the suspected reason, a doctor should be consulted. Gradual change, like becoming a little slower or forgetful, or tending to repeat information, can be a natural consequence of growing older and, providing it does not adversely affect the person's life style or safety, should not be a cause for concern.

On the other hand, brain failure or dementia is serious and irreversible. There are two kinds of dementia. The first is caused by the narrowing of the arteries in the brain, reducing the blood supply. As we have seen, this can cause blockages which lead to strokes, but it can also cause smaller failures in different parts of the brain, like little lights going out. The deterioration is thus not as dramatic as with a stroke, although someone with arteriosclerotic dementia is quite likely to suffer a stroke. Reducing the blood pressure helps, but there is no way of treating the condition itself.

The second form of dementia remains a mystery – cells

degenerate but the cause is not known and, sadly, the condition cannot be treated. When brain failure of this kind affects elderly people (though it can strike younger age groups too) it is sometimes termed senile dementia. Most old people do not suffer from senile dementia and anyone whose mind appears less fit than usual should not assume that it is the onset of dementia.

Health Services

Elderly people are notoriously reluctant to take up services and benefits to which they are entitled. Many find it difficult to separate in their own minds the modern state-financed services from the charity and *largesse* of earlier times. Understandably they do not want to take action which could threaten their independence, and even just asking for help can be seen in that light.

All this is a pity – to regard any statutory service as a charity is to misunderstand its function and to ignore one crucial difference: these services are provided as a right, not as a privilege. Even when the service is supposedly discretionary, rules dictate who is entitled to receive it. As for not wishing to seek help for fear of losing independence, the quickest way to become dependent is to allow matters to get worse without asking for assistance.

The principal health care 'organisation' in the United Kingdom is, of course, the National Health Service. It is a large, complicated enterprise and it is hardly surprising that most people find its personnel confusing and its structure incomprehensible.

Although it is known as a national service, the NHS is run by health authorities in each locality. The main contribution of national government is to distribute money to these authorities. In England, for example, there are two levels of authority – Regional Health Authorities are responsible for long-term planning, while the smaller District Health

Authorities run all the major services and hospitals and employ nearly all NHS staff. Each District is organised into units which can be individual hospitals, groups of hospitals or community services.

General practitioners are in a rather different category. They are not employees of the NHS but independent contractors. For this reason any difficulty with a GP or an application to change doctor should be referred to the Local Family Practitioner Committee (the address of which should be listed in the telephone directory).

No one would wish to advocate wasting a doctor's valuable time, but, particularly when you are older, it is important not to hesitate to seek medical advice. There is no shame attached to being told that all is well and GPs are paid to give reassurance and encouragement as much as they are to dispense pills.

The same applies to doctors in hospitals – they are often overworked and under pressure, but that should not prevent patients and their relatives from securing the information they require. The senior medical figure in the hospital setting is the consultant. He has beneath him senior registrars and registrars and the junior appointments are known as house officers or housemen. All are fully qualified doctors. If in any doubt, every patient is entitled to ask to see the consultant responsible for his or her care.

If anything, nurses and nursing can appear more confusing than the doctors – hospital patients are usually faced with an array of uniforms certain to baffle all but the most determined investigator. There are two grades of qualified nurses in the UK: enrolled nurse (EN or SEN as it used to be known) and registered general nurse (RGN or, until recently, SRN). Enrolled nurses undergo a two-year training and cannot hold the more senior posts. RGNs have completed three years of training, after which they can hold a staff nurse's post. Many of those around the ward will be young nurses in training and usually they have symbols on their uniforms to indicate what stage they have reached. Pupil nurses are those on an enrolled nursing course and student nurses are being trained to be RGNs. The key figure remains the Sister or charge nurse. District nurses, who work in the community, are fully qualified nurses who have done additional training. Although they operate in close liaison with GPs and often the doctor will arrange for them to call, the district nursing service is run by the health authority and can be contacted directly. (The service should be listed under 'Nurse' in the telephone directory). It is also worth remembering that district nurses are trained to advise on many practical and emotional difficulties, as well as dealing with physical problems.

In hospitals and in the community, health authorities employ nursing auxiliaries. They are untrained staff who work under the supervision of qualified nurses. They can help with dressing, bathing and washing, and in the community auxiliaries are sometimes used to help frail or disabled patients to get into bed in the evenings or rise in the mornings.

It is possible to obtain private nursing from any one of a number of agencies, although this can be very costly. In almost every case it is sensible to explore what the NHS can do, except of course in the unlikely event that private health insurance covers a home nursing service. Where private nursing is required, the qualifications of the nurse should always be ascertained. Any one in doubt can check that a nurse is registered by contacting the United Kingdom Central Council for Nursing, Midwifery and Health Visiting. A nurse who is not on the register should not be employed.

In addition to nurses and doctors, there are many other health professionals, each with their own area of expertise. Occupational therapists, long mistakenly associated with the making of baskets, are trained to help patients adapt to disability by teaching them new skills which will re-establish independence or at least minimise dependency. Their main skills lie in helping people relearn how to dress, wash, cook and to regain confidence to undertake these vital activities of daily life. Occupational therapists are not necessarily expert cooks – they are skilled in minimising disability and they use these everyday activities, and others, to achieve that end. They are trained for three years, divided between college and practical training in hospitals and in the community. Unlike other health professions, occupational therapists in the community are mostly employed by local authorities and they work in social services or social work departments.

Apart from a few four-year degree courses, physiotherapists also train for three years. They are the experts in mobility and use exercises and manipulation to restore and maintain function. Like occupational therapists, they can advise on walking aids and they often visit patients' homes before discharge to assess whether they are ready to manage on their own in the community.

Sadly, there are still not enough community physiotherapists but it is always worthwhile finding out whether such a service exists. In some areas, GPs can refer directly to the hospital physiotherapy department, but in others it is necessary to go through a hospital consultant.

Private physiotherapy is readily available but, as with chiropodists, it is important to check the credentials of the individual concerned – the letters which indicate proper qualifications are MCSP (Member of the Chartered Society of Physiotherapy) or SRP (State Registered Physiotherapist). To check whether a practitioner is registered, contact should be made with the Council for the Professions Supplementary to Medicine.

An increasing number of people are turning to so-called alternative medicine and it is fair to say that unorthodox therapies have a long and distinguished tradition. Nurses and doctors are becoming much more ready to acknowledge the role of many of these practitioners and indeed some, such as osteopaths and chiropractors, have been more or less accepted for some time. It seems likely that in a few years many treatments now regarded as 'alternative' will be accepted by conventional medicine. Already acupuncture, dismissed as quackery or peripheral a couple of decades ago, is accepted as a proven therapy. Alternative medicine is thus becoming 'complementary' to orthodox treatments.

Caution is still the best policy – there are inherent dangers in embracing every remedy or theory that comes along. People thinking about approaching alternative therapists should try to find out if other people have benefited from a course of such treatment and should let their GP know what they intend to do.

Good health care is a right in this country and poor service should be reported. Professionals, by definition, are expected to maintain certain standards and serious failure to do so should result in the matter being referred to the appropriate professional body.

In the NHS any complaint that is not dealt with satisfactorily should be referred to the local Community Health Council. These were established as part of the NHS structure to represent patients and the community at large. There are some variations in the way they operate, but if they do not take up individual cases of complaint they will advise on how to conduct them. Two voluntary organisations may also help: the Patients' Association or the College of Health.

If the complaint is not a clinical matter and the health authority do not appear to have dealt with it adequately, the Health Service Commissioner or Ombudsman may investigate on a patient's behalf. He can be contacted directly or through a Member of Parliament.

4 Income in Retirement

By Evelyn McEwen

Retirement can last for twenty to thirty years. No one can be sure exactly how much they will need to spend as the years go by, but everyone can have a clear idea of their retirement income. The fixed nature of that income will be calculable, but inflation makes a marked effect on purchasing power if it swings violently. Low rates of inflation mean that the price of goods does not go up but the return on savings is low. High rates of inflation, as happened in the early 1970s in Britain, mean that the return on investment is good but the price of goods in the shops and of essential services rockets. Savings that have been made over a lifetime then seem valueless and an element of bitterness will creep in about the value of the years spent going without.

Be positive. Income at retirement is only fixed at the core. There are many ways to maximise income by the right decisions on pensions, investment, use of assets and a thorough knowledge of all the benefits available from the State through a supplementary pension, housing benefit and grants to maintain one's home. Your employer or the local education authority may run pre-retirement classes which will help clarify the situation on retirement income. Further information on this can be obtained from the Pre-Retirement Association.

Four months before your 65th birthday (60 if you are a woman) the Department of Health and Social Security (DHSS) will send you a pension claim form. At that stage, or before if you wish, the local social security office will be able to tell you your pension record. The total pension will include the basic State pension, elements of the graduated pension which ended in 1975, and of the newer additional or earnings related pension. The DHSS publish a general leaflet called 'Retiring' FB6, and if you want to work out the situation for yourself, books like *Your Rights*, published by Age Concern England, take you through the process step by step and are invaluable in pointing out other sources of income in retirement. Broadly, for those who have paid full national insurance contributions, a minimum pension is payable after a quarter of a working life which is 16–65 for men (60 for women), and a maximum after nine-tenths. If you are married with a wife who will be under 60 when you retire, you will receive a dependent wife's addition to your pension. Once she is 60 she will receive her own pension book for the same amount. If she has been paying the full national insurance stamp, she will receive a pension in her own right. If it is lower than the dependent's level it will be made up once her husband takes his pension. The advantage of the independent pension is that the wife can then qualify for wife's earned tax allowance in her own right for that part of the pension to which she contributed, whereas if it is a dependent's pension it can only be part of the married couples' tax allowance.

On top of the State pension, some people will have an occupational pension, either a company pension where both they and their employer have paid contributions to the fund or a personal pension plan which they have taken up as self-employed or because their workplace did not offer such cover. Now is the time for those who have worked for several employers, and most people have, to find out how much pension has been left in other funds from past employment. If contact is difficult because companies have moved or even gone out of business, the Occupational Pensions Advisory Service, who can be contacted through Citizens' Advice

Bureaux (CABs) may be able to trace them and can help with particular queries. Details about the value of your pension can be obtained from the personnel officer, pension trustee or trades union representative. Important decisions have to be made about what should be done with the money. In company schemes, one and a half times final salary can be taken as a lump sum which is tax free, and the rest put into a pension. In some schemes it will be the time to make a decision about the balance between the survivors' benefit and how much to take while both spouses are alive. For those people who have a personal pension plan which reaches maturity on retirement, it is possible to take three times the pension which would remain after the lump sum is taken. Similar decisions will also have to be made about survivors' benefits.

Decisions about the balance between lump sum and pensions are important as they can affect entitlement to other benefits. There is such a thing as a 'pensioner poverty trap', when income and savings in retirement stop people qualifying for benefits or reduce them so that every extra pound of income can lead to cuts in benefits. It is not possible to state limits to the poverty trap – life would be so much easier if it were – it will vary depending on the needs of the individual; but broadly speaking, no supplementary pension can be obtained if one has savings over £3,000, and those who have income which is up to about £50 higher than the basic State pension level are likely to be affected by the trap.

To understand this, it is necessary to look at the main ways in which the State supplements income in retirement. A supplementary pension is available for those people whose income is so low that they do not have enough to cover basic needs. This can be defined as the basic pension plus water rates: if they are over 65, a sum for heating, and for owner occupiers some support towards maintaining the home to cover repairs and insurance. Most people will need this amount, and if their income does not match it they will get a supplementary pension. Others may qualify for even more support towards heating, if their house is exceptionally difficult to heat or has an expensive central heating system, or they are very handicapped. They may also qualify for a special diet or laundry service. All these are factors which might not affect newly retired people but could be important later on. General information on this can be obtained in leaflets SB1 and SB8 from public libraries or the local social security office. People who are eligible for a supplementary pension are entitled to free dental treatment and free NHS glasses. They may also get help with one-off payments for special needs such as moving house, if their savings are below £500.

Everyone can get help with paying rates if their income is below a certain level. This is done through the housing benefit scheme administered by the local housing authority. This scheme also helps to pay the rent for council, housing association or private tenants. Details about the way in which the scheme operates can be obtained from your local council. It is well worth exploring this because there can be rebates higher up the income scale than one might suppose. Basically the scheme is calculated on a sliding scale, assessing income against rent and rates. All income is taken into consideration except for a small disregard for earned income, but not pensions unless they are industrial disability or war widows' pensions.

All income from savings is taken into account, although increases in National Savings certificate value are ignored. Adults living with you will be expected to contribute a certain amount. It is always important to check the details of schemes. There are special allowances for the handicapped and some councils will also disregard all war pensions.

Finding out about one's rights can be difficult. The most common source of information is the Citizens' Advice Bureau of which there are 900 throughout the country. There may be local welfare advice or money advice centres in your area. Ask at the council offices or the local library for details.

Inevitably, any scheme which matches income against need will mean that additional income leads to loss of benefit. The following table shows the complicated situation at the end of 1983 for people paying weekly rent of £12.32 and rates of £4.50.

£ weekly

Income single person	rent rebate	rate rebate	income tax	basic spending power
basic pension only	12.32	4.50	—	34.10
basic pension plus occupational pension of:				
£5	9.79	3.65		34.24
£10	7.36	2.68		35.84
£20	5.26	1.98	2.60	40.44
£40	1.05	0.58	8.60	48.84

The basic pension which was £32.59 in those days gave an entitlement of £1.51 supplementary pension covering the water rate. As can be seen, the trap deepens for those who are also brought into tax.

When Income is Less than Desired Expenditure

1   *Before Retirement*
People can plan for the future while still earning, by making decisions that will increase the amount of money available to them in retirement. Look first at the State pension scheme. Sometimes calculations will show that either husband or wife has inadequate contributions to guarantee a full pension.

Decide how valuable it would be to make up contributions. This can be done up to two years after a deficient or non-contributory year. Your local social security office will have leaflet NI 42 on this. If a wife has been paying a full stamp and gave up work to look after an elderly or disabled person in receipt of an attendance allowance, she might be eligible for Home Responsibility Protection and should claim this as it will protect her pension rights.

If she is still paying the married women's reduced rate contributions, calculate if there would be any advantage in changing to the full contributions, if she will have worked on this basis for at least eleven years before retirement. This includes full contributions in earlier years before marriage and therefore not many years may be needed to gain a pension. If the wife is older than her husband, remember that until he is 65, if she has no pension in her own right, she will receive nothing, even if she is over 60.

There is an option for those who have occupational and personal pensions, to increase the contributions that they make to the pension scheme. This can have the added advantage of reducing taxable income which could be especially helpful for those paying higher tax rates. Most occupational pension schemes must be funded at a set rate by both the employer and employee, but it is possible for the employee to make additional voluntary contributions up to 15 per cent of pensionable income at any time – the earlier it is done, of course, the more it will yield in final income. Men and women who have personal pension plans can put $17\frac{1}{2}$ per cent of net relevant earnings into a scheme up to the age of 50. This can be increased to 20 per cent from then on.

These decisions can be difficult to make twenty years before retirement, because personal desire to change jobs or the possibility of company closures can make the future uncertain. Most people begin to look seriously at this option within five to ten years of retirement. It may be worth taking out pension annuity such as this, even late in working life, to gain the tax relief and achieve some additional income for retirement.

At any stage, additional life assurance can help to increase income. Many people take out policies when they are young which will mature when they need them. It is still possible to take out such policies in later life, but there is now no tax relief and it is a better bet to increase pension contributions wherever possible. However, the first £1,500 of the surrender value of a life assurance policy is not regarded as savings for supplementary benefit purposes. Buying assurance while still at work produces a lump sum on retirement which becomes an annuity to supplement income. A life policy can also have the advantage of providing cover for dependents if the assured person dies while still working. It can also give flexibility when deciding how to take the pension option. The husband might take the occupational pension on his life, using the value of the insurance policy to provide an annuity for his wife on his death. It will be possible for contributions to cease on retirement with the policy continuing to accrue bonuses until his death.

Over 50 per cent of people in Britain own their own home. Most will have paid off the mortgage, some are still living in rented property, but, where the option exists to buy, it could be worth considering, as tax relief exists on mortgage interest payments. Interest on a mortgage can be included in a supplementary pension and some building societies are also offering interest only mortgages. Both methods ensure that on death or moving, the capital element can be repaid from the value of the property, but it does mean that there will be an asset which will almost certainly increase in value faster than any form of savings.

Owning one's own home also means that there is less chance of being caught in the poverty trap created by housing benefit for those who have to pay rent in retirement. Most people who live in council or housing association property will now have the right to buy their home on favourable terms. These range from 32 per cent less on the cost price if you have lived there for two years to 60 per cent less for 30 years. This ensures that on resale the family have an even greater asset, and after five years no part of the discount has to be repaid. The Department of the Environment issue a leaflet on the Right to Buy which can be obtained at CABs, local councils or housing advice centres.

2   *Working as an Option*

Anyone who continues to work beyond their official retiring age obviously reaps income benefit, but this can be surprisingly low when all factors are taken into consideration. It is foolish not to investigate the situation thoroughly; working for pennies appeals to very few. For those who work on, there are no longer national insurance contributions to pay but two options – take the pension now or let it lie and receive additional income when you finally retire. Those who take their pension now must consider the earnings rule which is operational for five years after the minimum state retirement age. This means that, if their income is above a certain level, basic pension will be gradually taken away until it eventually disappears entirely. The pension for a dependent wife will be affected by her earnings at the same level when she is over 60, but below that she can earn even less before the pension is cut. Therefore, for those who continue to hold down a reasonably well paid job, say two thirds of the national average or more, it is probably of little value to take the pension. Details of the rule and current rates are available in leaflet NI 196 from social security offices. After the age of 70 for men (65 for women) you can earn as much as you like and still receive all your state pension.

The pension can be left in for five years after the minimum

age and there will be increments of about an extra $7\frac{1}{2}$p in the £ a year on the basic pension. Increments can also be earned on graduated pension and the additional pension of 1p in the £, and this also applies to part of your occupational pension. Ask about the occupational pension element as this may pay out at a higher rate. Careful thought must be given to this decision, since it may be that the value of increments for those long years of work will be partially swallowed up in future through loss of benefit – the pensioner poverty trap again. All the details about options and current rates are available in leaflets NI 92 and NP 32.

Any calculation of total income must take into account the tax situation. For those over 65 there is a special age allowance which gives a high allowance, for single people and married couples, compared to younger people. This is valuable in allowing more disposable pre-tax income, but there is a ceiling. Beyond about twice the basic level the special age allowance is reduced until it disappears entirely. This creates its own trap – a tax rate of 50 per cent instead of 30 per cent between the lower and upper limits.

To work on, taking income and losing tax concessions, must be carefully considered and leaflet IR 4a will give the current rates. IR 4 explains the general position about taxation and the pensioner. These are available from the Inland Revenue or at local CABs. It may be that both men and women would be better, rather than working on at the same rate, to take a less well paid and strenuous job or work part time for additional income without losing pension benefits or tax allowances.

Looking for another job can be difficult at this age but, aside from Job Centres, there are a few other sources of advice: Success after 60 and REACH (the Retired Executives Clearing House) are two that specialise in the age group. In addition, some Age Concern and community groups run their own employment bureaux and the Employment

Fellowship has some schemes where a little money can be earned.

3   *In Retirement*

Once in retirement, there are two other major ways to provide additional income: the judicious investment of savings and the use of assets, be it capital or property, to buy an annuity.

Many books, such as *Your Taxes and Savings in Retirement*, describe ways to invest money. For personal advice those with sufficient capital can approach a broker or their bank manager, who will be happy to handle their portfolio. The London Stock Exchange will send you a list of stockbrokers in your area, as will BIBA (The British Insurance Brokers Association) and NASDIM (National Association of Security Dealers and Investment Managers).

Most people have limited savings, and financial advisors are not particularly interested in their problems. Some banks will now give consultations at an hourly rate rather than go on a percentage basis, but the best source of individual advice is undoubtedly the newspapers. Some run money pages which are very helpful, as do magazines such as *Choice*, the magazine for leisure and retirement planning. All papers regularly give figures about returns on investments, but there are a few considerations which people must take into account when deciding what to do with any savings they have. The first is whether the income from the investment will be taxable. If your income is so low that you will not pay tax, there is only one suitable place for investments where tax is not deducted at source and therefore irrecoverable. This is the Post Office – be it national savings, investment accounts or 'granny bonds'. Study the rate of returns currently obtaining and do not leave money from year to year without rethinking your position. Bank managers often see money left on deposit for many years which could be providing better returns if invested elsewhere.

Building society shares and bank deposit accounts may not be a good bet financially because of the tax situation – but they can yield advantages in other ways. They can be the best place to invest for liquid capital, since money tied up in savings bonds may only yield best results if it is left in for years, and money may be difficult to retrieve quickly in an emergency. Always find out how long it will take to obtain the money, and if there will be a charge on early encashment or a loss of bonus or basic interest. There are always advantages in keeping a minimum amount in a bank account, to avoid paying bank charges.

Other investments such as local authority bonds and gilt edged Government bonds can be purchased at council offices or post offices and are designed as fixed term investments. It is best to calculate how long you will want to leave the money in, how much you can afford and to choose a maturity date which will suit your requirements. Both have fixed interest rates, and in the case of Government bonds the nominal value on which interest is calculated may be different from the cost of bonds on purchase, which will affect the true interest rate.

If you have sufficient capital to do this, such investments can be a very attractive proposition, as can a little more playful dabbling in stocks and shares. Think about this – many Local Education Authorities run courses on 'The Stock Exchange and the small investor'. It may be that the leisure years of retirement will reveal a hidden talent which can be both an enjoyable hobby and bring in additional income into the bargain.

Leaving something to one's children is deeply ingrained in the British character. Today that something of value tends to be the home. Yet the home itself can be used as part of retirement income. A decision needs to be made on how long to stay in the family home where the children grew up, and when it is time to move into smaller accommodation. Choosing the right time will include considering the maximum value that can be obtained for the house, when smaller accommodation has other attractions for health reasons or cost of maintenance. It is a question of careful balance, but the additional capital realised from, say, five more years in a larger home, may outweigh the additional cost of upkeep during those years.

Even the house itself can be partially 'remortgaged' to provide an annuity. Various schemes are now on the market such as 'home income plans' and 'home reversion schemes' whereby, provided that one is over a certain age, a proportion of the value of the property can be turned into an annuity, repaid when the annuitant dies or gives up the home. This is usually only available for people over 70, or when the combined age of spouses is over 150 years. The maximum loan is usually between 60–80 per cent of the market value of the home. Again, taking an annuity could affect entitlement to a supplementary pension or housing benefit. Age Concern England publish a fact sheet, *Raising an Income on Your Home*, which gives details about financial institutions currently offering such a service.

Expenditure in Retirement

On retirement, many people's incomes drop by at least a half. Planning for this change in circumstances, and recognising what one's true situation is, will require careful examination. This may not be as dramatic as at first supposed, since some outgoings will reduce or disappear on retirement – national insurance and occupational pensions contributions, mortgage payments and, of course, less tax will be paid.

The figures opposite come from the Family Expenditure Survey 1982. The traditional 'pensioner' household is reliant for at least three quarters of its income on State pension and benefits. It is interesting to map out these and other costs of living from the survey which can be found in most good public library reference departments. Statistics will be out of

LOST OUTGOINGS

One man/one woman household 1982 £

	Pensioner household	Other retired household	Non-retired
Income Tax	0.26	12.20	31.71
NI Contributions	—	0.81	10.04
Life Assurance and pension contributions	0.84	1.29	8.13
Mortgage payments	—	2.30	17.42
TOTAL	1.10	16.60	67.30

SOME ITEMS OF EXPENDITURE

One man/one woman household 1982 £

	Pensioner households	Other retired households	non-retired
housing	13.13	22.68	24.25
fuel, light, power	7.11	8.60	7.75
food	19.77	23.16	26.91
alcohol	2.24	4.10	6.77
tobacco	2.00	2.41	3.96
clothing	3.68	6.48	8.84
durable housing goods	2.52	6.80	11.85
fares	0.55	0.62	2.26
running a car	2.33	6.61	11.43
post/telephone	1.51	2.31	2.44
entertainment	1.61	1.98	2.45
holidays, subscriptions	1.62	6.31	7.93
Total expenditure recorded net of income tax and insurance	65.16	107.10	141.57

date, but the Employment Gazette will give you the crude multiplier needed to add the rate of inflation to reach the current situation. Even if the pattern of your spending does not match the average exactly – and rarely will anyone's – it could be amusing, if not instructive, to compare yourself with this picture.

This chart shows clearly where you will inevitably spend more proportionately in retirement and where you might like to but be unable to do so. Food and fuel become a dominant factor. Paying for heating becomes a major worry to pensioners, particularly in the winter quarter. Staying at home more, and feeling the cold more, inevitably mean that more heating has to be used, and some pensioners will say that they regard keeping warm as more important than eating. Financial help is only available to people in receipt of a supplementary pension, but the size of the bills for such items as telephone, television licence or rates can become a frightening prospect. Today, many different methods exist to spread the payment of bills throughout the year – this is very important for heating – and range from stamps to monthly instalment plans. Some depend on payment in advance, so that those with better income have a double advantage as they can wait until the last moment to pay, leaving the money in their own accounts to gather interest.

Planning to lead an active life in retirement can be expensive. Hours of leisure pursuits can mean increased costs and it is well worth finding out about special concessions in sports centres and for further education and leisure classes. Spending on holidays may have to drop dramatically and, worst of all, a reduced income may mean a very careful look at car journeys. It may even mean giving up running a car just when mobility may be restricted. Any discussion amongst pensioners about the difficulties encountered in their lives, be it to obtain services, go shopping or enjoy leisure pursuits, always centres on the two major problems: lack of income and lack of mobility. The two are inextricably linked as public transport becomes less available because of the extent of private car ownership.

How to Reduce Expenditure

1 *Before Retirement*

Mr Micawber said, 'Annual income twenty pounds, annual expenditure nineteen, nineteen and six, result happiness. Annual income twenty pounds, annual expenditure twenty pounds nought and six, result misery.' Having looked at ways of maximising income, the final sum may still look gloomy and therefore it will be necessary to look at ways of reducing expenditure – the sooner the better.

For many people, the years before retirement are the most prosperous; maximum salary, wife out at work, children no longer financially dependent, or even living at home and contributing to the family. Now would be the time to make essential purchases before income drops. Consider the essential items that will be needed to see one happily through retirement in the most economic way. It may be wise to pay off the mortgage early and put equivalent sums into voluntary contributions for a pension.

Having too much capital can affect entitlement to supplementary benefit. Now may be the time to purchase a new car using some savings which may bring them below the limit.

The home should be looked at to make sure that all the major labour-saving devices have been bought and cost-saving measures taken. Consider economical heating systems, double glazing and insulation; leaflets are available from gas and electricity boards and you should calculate the cost of all appliances. Don't economise to the point of danger with ill-lit stairs and cold rooms. Insulation grants towards the cost of loft insulation may be best left until you have retired, since the value of the grant is higher for pensioners – but again this is a careful decision, taking into account savings for this against heating bills and the cost of materials. Remember that all grants mean an additional payment from your own pocket. Ask your council for the leaflets *Some Money on Loft Insulation* and *Home Improvement Grants*, which now and in retirement can help to take worry out of maintaining your home.

2 *In Retirement*

Maintaining a home in retirement may be one of the biggest worries. It can often result in people unnecessarily allowing their home to deteriorate or moving because they cannot cope – neither may be necessary. There is a collection of State grants which can help to pay for improvements and major repairs. For houses built or converted before 1961 there are Intermediate and Improvement Grants. The former is a mandatory grant towards basic amenities – inside toilet, hot and cold running water and a bath; the latter will pay towards major improvements and any associated repair work. Improvement grants are discretionary and have rateable valuable ceilings. So do repairs grants which are available for pre-1919 property to pay for major structural repairs such as roofs, walls and foundations. This can be very useful if the home was in good repair at retirement but twenty years on, like its owner, shows signs of age. Environmental Health Officers located at your local council are most helpful about advising on grants and procedure. They will also help if you are living in someone else's property which needs work done. If help cannot be obtained through a grant, loans may be obtained through the local council, building society or bank, and are subject to tax relief for some home improvements. The property can be remortgaged and, increasingly, building societies offer maturity loans on the strength of its value. Thus a lump sum can be obtained through them, only interest has to be paid (which we have seen may be covered by a supplementary pension for essential work) and the capital is repaid on death or if a person moves house.

Moving may be an option to reduce expenditure because the house is expensive to run or is far away from shops and amenities so that travel costs are high. Other factors may enter into the decision. Finance will never be the sole consideration but it is advisable to write down all expenses when contemplating such a move, and compare them with the new situation.

Shopping is another major expense. Retirement can mean more time to shop around for bargains. It can also mean less energy to want to do so. Look at your buying and eating habits. Purchase of a deep freeze or a fridge freezer helps to purchase in bulk and cook more cheaply, and cash-and-carry stores can help such purchases. These can be shared with friends. Some Age Concern clubs have schemes to sell essential items at cost price.

Look carefully at your diet predominantly for its nutritive value, but also with a careful eye on cost. A boiled egg may do you far more good than a rump steak and cost far less. Eating habits of a lifetime can not only be bad but expensive. There are a number of books on diet; a useful one is Louise Davies' *Easy Cooking for One or Two*. Savings can be made not only in buying food but in cooking it. The freezer pizza may seem a reasonable buy, but when the instructions say cook in a 400° oven for 30 minutes, the cost can be out of proportion. Slow cooking pots or pressure cookers can make savings.

Continuing to run a car may be particularly difficult in retirement. This is where careful purchasing of a model which is economical to run and easy to maintain is valuable. *Motoring Which?* regularly looks at such factors. Don't forget about the mobility allowance if you are very disabled before the age of 65 (the allowance can be claimed up to the age of 66). It can help to pay for taxis or to run a car either through your own payment or involvement in the Motability scheme until you are 75. The allowance is not taxable and leaflet NI 211 gives detailed information. Motability have a scheme which helps to purchase or lease a car with the mobility allowance.

What makes the difference for many people in retirement is the chance to get away from it all and have a holiday; yet this, as we have seen, may normally only be available to those who have reasonable occupational pensions. There are, however, any number of opportunities for cheaper holidays. Go at the right time with companies such as SAGA holidays for the over 60s, and in the winter off-peak, two months in Spain can cost as little as two weeks in high summer. It can also save home expenses, particularly that of heating the house during a cold British winter. Many companies offer such packages which usually have their own couriers, entertainment and built-in procedure if you should fall ill while away. Some voluntary and self-help groups also arrange holidays. Belonging to a widows' club or Age Concern group can lead to a low price holiday. There may even be an opportunity for a subsidised holiday for those on a very limited income, particularly if they need the rest and change through ill health. Enquire at your local council social services office to see if they can help to pay for a holiday or can point you to a voluntary association who can or who organise such holidays.

When to Retire
Continuing to enjoy holidays is all part of the fun of retirement, making it happen because you can if you want to. So far we have looked at the general picture of retirement income and expenditure, but life does not progress at a continuous, even tenor.

For many people retirement is a matter of choice, but for some it may be brought about through redundancy, unemployment or ill health. Each circumstance demands a separate set of decisions about the future. Choosing when to retire must be done slowly and carefully. Take time to make the right decision, based not only on the wish for leisure and more time with the family, but with knowledge of how much income you will have.

Those who plan early retirement usually have an occupational pension which will tide them over until the State pension age. The pension itself will be actuarially reduced unless the company pension age is lower than the State minimum pension age. Calculation then has to be made about additional income support that may be forfeited because of the occupational pension. The poverty trap factors have already been mentioned, but there are additional points to consider. A year's unemployment benefit will be forfeited if the occupational pension is over a certain level and its recipients over 60. Ironically, anyone under 60 does not suffer this loss. The position is explained in leaflet NI 30. There is no flexibility within the State system for reduced pensions at a lower age, or for part pension/part work schemes which will allow for gradual retirement. Some employers have such schemes, but they are still few and far between. The only State help which can give a boost to income is the Job Release Scheme, which was designed to provide younger people with jobs. Thus it is possible for older people to give up their jobs for someone on the unemployment register and obtain a weekly payment which is above the level of the pension. This is only available towards the end of a working life. Details are available from Job Centres, Employment Offices or Unemployment Benefit Offices, or on leaflets PL 741 and PL 728. Changes occur regularly, so that it would never be wise to rely on information a few months out of date.

Happy retirement is increasingly giving place to forced retirement through redundancies, and the realisation among people over 55 that they may never work again. People caught in this situation often feel more depressed than pensioners and find that they have less to live on. There are pitfalls here which must be considered – lump sum redundancy payments, though tax free, may bar people from supplementary benefit and limit housing benefit. Unemployed people can get support for their dependents, but if they are working it could affect the benefit. Full details are in leaflet NI 12. For the first year, unemployment benefit is obtainable for those with full contribution but, thereafter, supplementary benefit is on a means tested basis and is only at the short term rate. This is less than the pension, unless one is over 60, when the long term rate is given if the person ceases to register for work and therefore accepts that retirement has come. If there is no opportunity for paid work and the income situation is bleak, there are now Community Programme schemes for those unemployed over a year, which can pay more than supplementary benefit, and are not subject to means testing. Information about this can be obtained at the local Job Centre which has a leaflet for the programme.

Sadly, one of the most common causes of early retirement is ill health. Those who have paid full national insurance contributions will receive a sickness benefit up to 28 weeks and thereafter an invalidity benefit which is paid until the age of 70 for men (65 for women). It is not taxable at present, and there are additional allowances for dependents. Anyone who is invalided for more than five years before the State pension age can receive an additional allowance. There are also allowances for dependents if they are not working or are on low incomes; the details are in leaflet NI 16A.

Company Occupational Pensions provide for those who have to retire early because of ill health. These are normally on favourable terms which waive the years of missing contributions and pay out on the agreed proportion of salary which has been reached.

Ill health is a burden that nothing can assuage, but there are benefits from the State which can help to make life more bearable. These include the mobility allowance and supplementary benefit, which as we have seen can pay for additional needs because of ill health. An Attendance Allowance is payable for those who have needed continuous care, either by day or night, for at least six months. Those who care for them can receive an Invalid Care Allowance if they are not married or a cohabitee. Leaflets NI 205 and NI 212 will give a general idea of these schemes. It can be invidious to undergo a medical test to qualify for such benefits, but once obtained they can make all the difference to remaining independent in the community. Don't give up if your claim is initially turned down; many people win through when they appeal further.

Living Alone

We tend to have a preconceived idea of what constitutes a family, but many people will have been single all their lives and others will be divorced or widowed in retirement. Single people often suffer because they have no one to turn to when they need help in handling their affairs, in arranging their funeral and handling their estates. It is therefore important to find and appoint someone who will agree to be responsible. This could be a solicitor, but if a non-formal support is required, the local Citizens' Advice Bureau may be able to help. Some single people live with their parents and should plan carefully if the home will eventually have to be sold to be shared between children.

Divorced people can encounter many difficulties particular to their situation. A Social Security Leaflet, NI 95, gives some information. Broadly, if you are divorced before 60 (65 if a man) the contributions of your ex-spouse count towards your pension, provided that you do not remarry. If you remarry after the minimum State pension age, you will not lose pension rights from a former marriage. Unfortunately, women who are only separated can only receive a lower rate of pension, and only when the husband draws his pension.

A major change will occur in any family with the death of a spouse. Frequently, the husband will die first. It is then essential that the widow obtains advice on her changed circumstances. Contrary to popular belief, there is no widows' pension for a woman widowed after 60, but there is an additional tax allowance in the year of the husband's death. Early application to the local Social Security Office will help sort out the pension entitlement, which will include the same level of basic pension as the husband, ie. half his graduated pension and all his additional pension. The local housing authority must be informed immediately to get an increase in housing benefit. The pension fund must be contacted to find out about survivors' benefit. The overwhelming difficulties faced at a time of bereavement can be helped by contacting CRUSE, the Association of Widows, who have local groups, or Age Concern groups which have bereavement counselling schemes. They can provide emotional support and practical help.

Ill health and death

1 *Ill Health*
Most people will continue in good health for many years. Some may remain in their own homes all their lives with very little or no additional help. Increasing old age may bring no additional demands on income, but ill health can lead to increased costs and important decisions about where and how to continue to live comfortably.

The National Health Service gives free treatment from general practitioners, district nurses and in hospitals. There is no charge for drugs or appliances and it is not necessary to pay for private health care. Nonetheless some elderly people do so, very often because of the length of Health Service waiting lists for some of the most common complaints of old age, such as the need for hip replacements. Some 16 per cent of all elective surgery outside the NHS is on people over 65. Most companies will not take on new clients in this age group, but Private Patients Plan will.

Which? magazine has published articles about the value of such schemes, but read the small print very carefully, since insurance may pay for acute care but not for a long stay.

Yet even with much free care there may be additional health costs. It is good to have sufficient income to decide whether to purchase more attractive spectacles, dentures, private chiropody and other services from complementary medicine, such as osteopathy or acupuncture. These are not normally provided on the Health Service.

Chronic Illness

45 per cent of people over 65 are chronically ill. This brings the need for other forms of support for those who want to remain in their own homes. There is provision under the terms of the Chronically Sick and Disabled Persons Act to provide adaptations around the home, stair rails and even a downstairs toilet. Most councils will charge for this work on a means tested basis. You can have a telephone installed. Ask at your local Council Social Service department for information and, if in doubt, contact RADAR, who advise people who feel they are not getting their rights.

Some people pay privately for help at home, but local councils do provide meals on wheels, home helps and even home care assistants who can get people out of bed, help them to dress, wash and cook meals. A charge may be made for the service but this, again, is usually related to income and, in some cases, councils give all such services free. If the local social service authority does not provide them, it is likely that there will be a voluntary agency in the area who will. Ask at your local Council of Voluntary Service or Rural Community Council.

A final expense which may be well worthwhile for those who do not want to move into sheltered housing or even residential care, is to be linked to an alarm system. This can counter the fear of being alone. The Disabled Living Foundation have a list of such schemes. Alarms may be worn as a 'bracelet' or 'necklace' and therefore about one's person, linked to a terminal so that emergency help can be raised from relatives, friends or the police. Sometimes it will be possible to link into a local housing authority who have an alarm scheme. There are also schemes to be linked to a peripatetic worker who would call if there was a crisis, but these may be charged for.

2   *Residential Care*

Sheltered housing is covered by the Housing Benefit scheme and the additional cost of warden service is included in the benefit. Where a more supportive form of care is thought desirable, for example in hospital, residential or nursing home, the financial situation is very complicated. It is worth thinking about this eventuality well in advance. 'Saving for a rainy day' is an old saying, but you may find that all your savings are used up to pay for care. People who find themselves in this situation feel resentful that those who have not saved are subsidised, while they have to pay. They are also left with less to leave their children than they expected.

For people with more income and savings than the basic State pension, the cheapest option for long stay care is the hospital or, if you are lucky enough to live in the right area, an NHS nursing home. Only the basic State pension is seen as income, after eight weeks it is reduced, and after a year all but a personal allowance is taken away. There is no regard to other income or to ownership of a house.

Residential care may be in local authority Part III homes or in private or voluntary homes under local authority sponsorship. In this case all income is taken into account and capital above £1,249 taken as income at the rate of interest of 26 per cent. This inevitably digs into savings. The value of the home is included, unless the spouse, a dependent child or a carer is left living there. If the spouse is living outside the home, his or her income may be assessed to help to pay for this care. Private residential and nursing home care can be paid for by Social Security through a similar system, except that no help can be given where there are savings above £3,000, and the rules on selling the home may be more stringent.

All these claims on assets can be made even if they were given away, if it can be proved that this was knowingly done, in order to evade charges. It is therefore essential for families to look well ahead, so that they are not caught unwittingly in the rules. These are explained in an Age Concern fact sheet, *Charges for Elderly People in Residential Accommodation.*

3 *Handling Money*

Many people fear what will happen if they are no longer able to handle their own affairs. Simple procedures can be used if there is only pension income, since Social Security benefits can be managed by an agent who signs the allowance book or by an appointee if money is to be handled regularly. Form BF 56 from the Social Security Office explains this procedure. Some occupational pensions can be sent to a relative, and there may be no need to use savings.

If there are more assets, or circumstances change, it may be necessary to seek legal powers. The most common is a Power of Attorney, which can be arranged through a solicitor so that someone such as a husband or daughter can manage one's affairs. Ask about free legal aid under the Green Form Scheme if you are on low income. A new form of 'Enduring Power of Attorney' now enables the power to be held even if the person becomes mentally incapacitated, provided it is agreed beforehand. If, however, the person is already incapacitated, an application should be made to the Court of

Protection. A receiver will be appointed by the Court to handle affairs. This is often a friend or a relative. Charges are made, but can be waived in cases of hardship. There is a less elaborate procedure where there is little money and then no charges. This is explained in leaflet PN 1, and the Court issues a general leaflet about its work.

4   Death

Most people would want to plan for their own death, if only they knew where to turn, because they do not want to leave their families with any problems. It is essential to make a will. If your assets are very limited and your bequests simple, you can do it yourself using a will form purchased cheaply from the stationers'. It must be witnessed by two people at the same time who must not be beneficiaries, and you should name an executor who will carry out your wishes, who can be a beneficiary. You should leave it in a safe place. Age Concern produce a leaflet, *Instructions for my Next of Kin and Executors Upon my Death*, which you can use to point out where all important papers are kept. They also issue a free fact sheet on *Making Your Will*.

It is possible to plan your own funeral. Insurance policies can be taken out to cover costs, and some funeral directors will arrange details in advance. The Life Offices Association may be able to tell you about insurance schemes, and the National Association of Funeral Directors about what their members will do. The DHSS publish leaflets D 49, *What to do After a Death*, and NI 49 which explains about the Death Grant which is still only £30, but helps towards the cost of a funeral.

You may wish to leave your body for medical research, but this is not always possible. Information about this can be obtained by writing to HM Inspector of Anatomy.

It is not uncommon for people to worry about their own funeral. It can be reassuring to know that, in straitened circumstances, if you die in hospital they will arrange burial and, if in the community, the Social Services have an obligation to arrange a simple funeral if there is no relative who can help. Relatives who are on supplementary benefit can be helped to pay for the funeral.

Planning ahead – saving for death as for life – can give a sense of satisfaction that one's affairs are in order. The pattern has been completed and the fear of an inadequate income will not mar the Adventure of Ageing.

5　House and Home

By Rose Wheeler

'Home sweet home', 'an Englishman's home is his castle' – these and many other expressions remind us of the importance of our home in creating comfort and happiness. We spend more waking hours in the home than anywhere else and, of course, more or less all of our sleeping hours. Memories are tied up in our home; the brickwork can become almost human with familiarity. Above all a home can contribute a sense of stability to our lives.

There are other reasons why a home is important. It is a permanent asset, so decisions about where to live and what type of house to live in have to be made with great care. The home has all sorts of responsibilities for the owner attached to it, such as home maintenance. For a growing number of people, it forms the major part of their inheritance. These, too, are important considerations. But above all, our home is usually the most costly item any of us have to pay for in our lives.

This chapter looks at the contribution housing can make to independence and comfort in later life. For those previously working outside the home, retirement means that the home itself may become the main focus of activity. Living alone for the first time often brings a new importance to where we live. As housing is an important influence in our lives, there are many ways in which we can make sure that this influence is a positive one. All too often poor, cold or unsuitable homes make life unnecessarily miserable. Later in this chapter we shall look at ways of ensuring that the home and environment bring comfort and independence rather than misery. But we look first at the problems that can occur which could be avoided with some forethought and planning. The main ones are barriers to independent living, keeping warm, and being free from anxiety about the home.

Independent Living

What are the worst barriers that housing can create for independent living? First of all, design. Architects who plan the layout and style of housing are usually young to middle-aged and sometimes unaware of the difficulties, such as restricted mobility, that may occur in later years. They also tend to be male, which may account for the often-heard complaints about kitchen design made by those who spend much of their time in the kitchen. The design of housing has also been influenced by its providers, both private builders and governments. Family housing – three bedrooms, two storeys, with the bathroom and toilet upstairs – is the type which has most frequently been constructed in the United Kingdom.

There are three particular problems for those who live on in this type of house when the children have grown up and moved away. First of all, it may be too big. We have yet to enter the age of flexible housing that can be adapted for different stages in our lives – for example, sections that can be safely and effectively sealed off when no longer required. Ample space can of course be an asset. It enables treasured pieces of furniture to be retained, and visitors such as relatives and friends to be accommodated. But space can also be a worry, since it can bring a number of disadvantages. The house is more difficult and more costly to heat and to clean. The rates may be higher than for a smaller home; so also is the cost of home maintenance and repair. And then there is a second set of problems tied to the particular features or design of a house. Perhaps the most daunting and widespread problems can occur in two-storey buildings, when climbing stairs becomes difficult. However, any danger or risk posed by stairs can be kept to a minimum by only using them when necessary and being careful. Those who have a downstairs toilet have less of a problem, but this convenience is rarely available and more commonly stairs have to be climbed with increasing regularity and sometimes speed as bodily functions become a little less efficient over the years. Unnecessary stress, indignity and, in some cases, dependence (for example, if a commode becomes necessary) can be caused by this single feature of house design. And if the stairs finally become impossible, the bed may be brought downstairs, too. The territory of 'upstairs' takes on a new meaning as a constant reminder of physical deterioration.

Other features of the home may also create dependence. The bath is a prime offender; even with secure rails at strategic points the bathroom can represent an anxiety and a risk, particularly for those who live alone. The thought of being stranded in the bath with no one at hand is an understandably worrying one. In 1981 over a third of people aged 75 or over, and nearly half of women in that age group in the United Kingdom, were living on their own, and the number is growing all the time.

Unless the home is one of the relatively few which have been designed with these problems in mind, numerous features can restrict our ability to live independent lives. Perhaps the power points can no longer be easily reached, necessitating help even for such simple tasks as vacuuming the carpet or unplugging the television. Then there are the letterbox, the milk bottles, and so on. For some people such problems are due to the house being unmodernised, perhaps even without an inside toilet. Proportionately more people aged over 65 than in any other age group, still have to cope with an all-weather route to the toilet, or instead suffer the indignity of a commode. 394,000 people of pensionable age in the United

Kingdom in the 1981 census were found to be without a toilet inside their homes. This represented one in 25 people in that age group, with a similar picture for those lacking a bath and piped hot water.

The third point is about the location of homes. The steep climb up the hill to the shops; the distance to the newly routed bus service; the distance from someone who could help in an emergency, from neighbours and relatives – all these things begin to matter much more once the agility of youth can no longer be taken for granted. There is a double disadvantage here. The only reason shopping is a problem may be climbing the steep hill to the shops. But in time, as a kindly neighbour or home help fetches the groceries, we may become less able to go shopping, becoming out of touch with prices and new products, and out of practice with selecting goods and getting value for money. So the environment – the home and its location – can be the root causes of dependence on others, and can make the situation worse by restricting independence in other ways, too.

Keeping Warm

There are difficulties here that, while they are less to do with the home – having thick curtains, adequate carpeting, using extra clothing or thermal underwear, electric blankets and so on – are still very important. So, too, is having enough money to pay for adequate fuel. But the size of the house and its state of repair, insulation and heating system, can often be the reason for cold living conditions.

We have already considered the problem of heating a home which has become too big once family members have moved away. But there are many reasons why a house may be unnecessarily cold. The front door may open from the street straight into the living room, or the back door into the kitchen. Without a porch, or double doors, a good deal of heat is lost every time the outside door has to be opened.

Disrepair is also a major reason for unnecessary heat loss or for cold air to creep in as draughts from outside. Rotting window frames, ill-fitting doors, crumbling cement between the bricks, a slate or tile missing from the roof, are all fairly common causes of draught and cold. Damp walls, too, create cold as they conduct heat out of the house. Quite minor repair problems, such as a cracked or broken gutter or drainpipe, can cause this. A more serious problem may be found in older homes which were built without a damp-proof course. It should be remembered that a larger proportion of older than younger people live in older houses which need attention.

Insulation measures, which are often an automatic feature of newly built homes, may never have been installed in older properties. The simplest and most effective measures are loft insulation and draught-proofing strips (for example fixed along the base of external doors). Still about one in four retired households have no loft insulation.

Trying not to let the heat out and the cold air in is one thing, but any such efforts will have a limited effect on warmth if the heating system is not producing adequate or efficient heat. The type of heating system used often depends on what people can afford. Fewer old people than any other age group have central heating (only about a half of retired households in 1981), yet studies have shown that gas central heating may be one of the cheapest types of heating to run. The use of individual heaters in different rooms, particularly electric bar fires, can entail greater expense while producing less warmth.

Without central heating, it is of course more difficult to keep the whole house warm, quite apart from being able to pay for it. The living room may be very cosy indeed, but the rest of the house virtually unheated. Moving from a very warm, to a cold room or corridor, is not a recipe for good health, and indeed having to do so may even discourage necessary physical activity. It may be very tempting to curl up in front of a warm fire and put off making a meal at the thought of a cold kitchen.

One heating system in particular can bring a whole host of problems and difficulties - solid fuel. Coal and other solid fuels need to be carried into the house from outside; fires need to be lit and kept going, and at the start of the day there are ashes to be swept and carried to the dustbin. Any ill health or frailty may make it difficult to carry coal or to bend down. Relying on someone else to be coal carrier and fire lighter is not uncommon. In some areas, teams of home helps carry out such a service. While some people may receive free coal because of past employment, and others may favour the rosy glow of an open coal fire, this does not detract from the fact that this is one form of dependency created by our homes. A push-button heating system would remove the need for help of that kind.

It hardly needs stressing why warmth is so important as we grow older. We spend more time at home; we are sometimes less active and, with chronic sickness, disability or frailty, older people, like young children, require additional and constant warmth. There is a hidden danger, too. The human body is itself a poor judge of its own warmth. One of the characteristics of hypothermia - the condition when the body temperature becomes dangerously low - is that people do not necessarily feel cold. So, unless there is a thermometer to help judge the level below which the temperature should not fall, the threat to health may not be at all obvious.

A Trouble-free Home

A final set of difficulties concerning everyday living in our homes, are the responsibilities that go with it. Much depends on the type of housing lived in. We look in turn, at renting from a private landlord, renting from the local council and, finally, owning a home.

In numerical terms, private landlords are a dying breed. But a high proportion of older people still rent from them. Many of these houses do not have modern amenities, and the state of repair may be less than satisfactory. While the landlord has a responsibility to maintain and improve the house or flat, many are reluctant to do so. Landlords may themselves be elderly. They may argue that they cannot afford, even with government grants, their share of the cost of work. They may lead tenants to believe that improvements or repairs, if carried out, will result in excessive rent rises. There may be confusion over responsibility for certain repairs, with the result that they are left undone. A tenant may be afraid to push for rightful repairs or improvements, for fear of souring relations with a landlord who lives on the same premises. In some, the only contact is through an estate agent and it can be extremely difficult to find out who is the landlord. Local authority tenants may also experience particular problems. The authority may recognise its responsibility to undertake repairs, but be extremely slow to act. In some local authorities, tenants are responsible for a number of basic repairs, for example, to toilet or kitchen fittings, which may be difficult to carry out, particularly for older people. Many councils, however, are sympathetic to the needs of older people and would not impose unrealistic responsibilities.

As a tenant in council, private or housing association accommodation, there are inevitably a number of restrictions. Pets may not be allowed. There may be no choice over the type of heating, and so on.

For owner occupiers the responsibilities that come with ownership may weigh more heavily as we get older. The maintenance, repair and improvement of the property has to be organised and paid for. By 1984, three out of every five homes were in home ownership, and some people have predicted that this will rise to at least four out of five by the end of the century. There may be little or no mortgage still outstanding by the time one has reached retirement, but the costs of repairs and maintenance are high, and often unpredictable. Little is allowed to meet these costs for those receiving supplementary pension.

If income or savings are insufficient, small repairs are often postponed or neglected for a time, and can lead to serious and costly repair problems. Many owners may not recognise the need for repairs in the first place. Widows, whose husbands saw to 'that side of things' when they were alive, are often ill equipped to look out for signs of neglect or to be aware of the maintenance tasks required, such as cleaning out the eaves spouts regularly. The current government, in encouraging people to buy their homes, is successfully selling council houses to sitting tenants whose average age – at 43 years – is already 12 years higher than that of other people buying a house for the first time. Yet being a home owner in later years may be particularly difficult. Climbing ladders and carrying out minor repair jobs may become a thing of the past, and for the majority who live on a state pension or supplementary benefit, there may not be enough money to pay for these jobs to be done.

Unlike tenants, owners may in theory be able to choose the most appropriate form of heating, but in practice, cost may prevent a choice being made. Government grants, as we shall see later, may sometimes be available for heating and home improvement, but what of the problems of organising work, dealing with the builders, and so on?

Where repairs or routine jobs such as exterior paintwork are neglected, for these and other reasons, anxiety may be made worse by knowing that the once tidy home appears to the outside world as dilapidated and uncared for. The appearance of the garden may become a further cause of anxiety. A large garden, designed with no thought of raised flower beds, may slowly become an eyesore and an embarrassment. It can also be upsetting to be reminded that the display of flowers that was once an annual pride and joy is now relegated to memory.

Whose Problems?

But all these problems and difficulties should not paint a uniform picture of gloom; many older people never experience any of them at all. Our concern, however, is with those people who do have first hand knowledge of some or all of those problems. If unsuitable, poor and cold housing conditions are unnecessary, or even avoidable, why do so many people continue to have to put up with them? The most important single explanation is the relatively low level of resources – both income and savings – on which many older people live. For those who have sufficient income through their working lives to plan a retirement free from housing problems, or who have an adequate store of savings to cover housing costs as they arise, housing may contribute to a satisfactory standard of living. But bearing in mind the limited incomes of many people, particularly those who rely on a State pension, it is worth seeing if there are ways of tackling or of avoiding certain housing problems. What help is available from government funds and agencies – both centrally and locally?

First of all, when should decisions about the home be made? For many people, problems with their homes only come to the fore when they are in their 70s or when they begin to be less active or mobile themselves. For some people, the home may never pose any of the problems discussed earlier. But there is no way of knowing how fortunate we will be. The only safeguard against ending up living in cold or unsuitable housing, when we are too frail to consider moving or improving the home, is to anticipate problems, then get advice, make carefully considered plans and carry them out, with help if necessary.

The expenses and permanence of housing are such that these decisions, made in early retirement, cannot (or should not) be made in haste. It will not be easy to change any plans once they take shape. For example, the decision to divide a large house into flats may become a disaster on discovering the unforeseen problems connected with becoming a landlord. Moving away from relatives and friends to the coast is the most well-known example of a major decision that can go badly wrong.

It is not just a question of making a choice between staying, or moving house. Making a move is not the end of the matter. There is no final decision or plan beyond which all concerns about the home can be forgotten. You may decide to sell your house to move to somewhere smaller; a few years later repairs are necessary; later, a sensible plan to improve the heating is carried out. After a few more years a stairlift is installed and the power points raised, and so on. Needs change and new needs arise. Preferences may alter as priorities and aspirations change. Relatives or close friends may move away; the once convenient bus route is changed; a partner dies, leaving you alone for the first time after many years of sharing a home and all the decisions that go with it.

With this continuity and flux in mind, how can we ensure, without limitless personal savings or income, that our home and the environment we live in remain suitable to our needs?

Creating a Satisfactory Home
There are four things in life that are worth striving for which housing can enhance or stifle. They are independence, comfort, warmth and safety. So far we have only considered how, in those four areas, homes hamper enjoyment of living. In this section we look at the measures and decisions that can be carried out to solve or avoid them and, in the final section, we look at how to carry out these plans and at what help is available in the United Kingdom.

Although in some cases independence may be more a state

of mind than the enjoyment of physical freedom, in this chapter we are only concerned with physical freedom. Stairs and steps, outside and upstairs toilets, baths, coal fires and low-level power points, were all identified earlier as prime offenders in creating difficulties for independent living. This should be of concern to policy-makers, too, in terms of the cost of providing what may be inappropriate resources. Home helps may come to light coal fires, health visitors to help people out of the bath or to empty the commode. They also help to keep an eye on elderly people as a friendly visitor, to provide a listening ear. Services compensating for problems caused by our housing could lead us, however, to undervalue our own capacities. Health visitors or home helps come and assist with certain tasks and, in turn, elderly people may become too dependent. Some social services departments in different parts of the United Kingdom have got this message. They understand the need for independence and provide many more services aimed at rehabilitation or 'getting people on their feet again'. The development of community occupational therapy is a good example. Occupational therapists are experts in helping people to relearn and develop the skills of independent living, using aids or adaptations, if necessary.

One recent study clearly demonstrated that decisions about services were made by professionals rather than the people themselves. In one case an elderly lady in a wheelchair had all her shopping collected for her by the home help. Yet, when asked, it was plain that what *she* wanted was to do the shopping herself, and all she needed was to be pushed to the shops and around the supermarket, in order to do so. The message is clear – to remain independent we must fight the passive acceptance of what professionals say we need. This is particularly relevant to housing. Professionals, such as social and housing workers, sometimes appear to be rather blinkered about the housing needs and problems of elderly people. One of the most common types of housing built especially for elderly people is sheltered housing and there has been, and in many areas still exists, a belief that sheltered housing is the answer if one's home becomes difficult to manage in any way, or is dilapidated or old. Sheltered housing consists of a group of dwellings built together. A warden normally lives on site and has a responsibility to answer emergency calls, to keep an eye on the occupiers, and to provide various services. There is usually an alarm system linking each unit to a central point, so that the warden or his/her relief is always on call if someone has a fall, or if there is an emergency. Whilst alarms are there for emergencies, they are more frequently used for all kinds of non-urgent requests and problems, than for real emergencies.

Some studies show that occupiers of sheltered accommodation have often been rehoused, simply because their previous home was unsuitable (ie. it needed repairs, improvements or adaptations of some kind). But 'sheltered housing' is still many people's notion of the ideal for elderly people. It may be the best solution for some people, but it has to be remembered that it can be a costly way of housing people. There are recent developments which enable alarm systems or warden services to be taken to ordinary homes in the community, avoiding the need for a move. A telephone may sometimes be just as useful. As few countries could ever hope to provide sheltered housing for all their elderly citizens, and if what is in fact required is better housing, then improving or adapting the house, or moving to a small single-storey house or flat, may be more appropriate and possibly a lot less costly for the country as a whole.

Many of the problems experienced in the home have to do largely with its design and any deficiencies it may have in terms of disrepair or missing amenities. Convincing older people that they have a special need for sheltered housing, rather than the need to improve their homes, implies that they have 'special' needs because they are old. They are then seen as 'special' rather than as individual members of the population who sometimes have different preferences or needs. Above all, elderly people have the same needs and rights to a decent standard of housing as the younger generation.

Using our home to maintain or enhance independence may involve us in quite a battle against accepted professional practice. Relatives and friends, for quite the best reasons, may be more concerned about relieving their own anxiety than considering an elderly relative's needs and wishes. This is particularly true when elderly people live alone.

Moving to sheltered housing provided by the local authority or a housing association may be one way of giving up the responsibility of home ownership. In most areas of the United Kingdom housing options are very limited and therefore choice tends to be restricted.

Since the early 1980s, sheltered housing units have become increasingly available in the private sector, either for sale or for leasehold occupation. This is a welcome development, extending the options available in this type of provision. The costs of maintaining the buildings and providing a warden service are met by the occupiers. In some cases these charges have escalated and occupiers have expressed understandable anxiety. You should remember that charges might increase in the future if services prove more costly than anticipated, as residents become increasingly frail.

Most studies have found that moving in later retirement can be a risky business. For some people it is a considerable trauma. With careful planning, problems can be kept to a minimum, but some people are always likely to suffer unfortunate consequences. A move, therefore, for whatever reason, should not be undertaken without careful thought. Ronald Blythe offers us his words of wisdom on the subject, using a rather negative view of residential care, in saying,

'One of the ways to avoid the old people's home is to learn how to stay in our own homes.'

Warmth, Comfort and Safety

Living independently is closely bound up with warmth and safety in the home. Some modern buildings are built with every regard to efficient and economical warmth – cavity walls, loft insulation, double glazing, together with gas central heating. But the majority of us live in older, much less efficiently heated and insulated homes. The problems identified earlier in the chapter indicate where some of the solutions lie. Adequate repair and maintenance, no damp, central heating (or at least additional heating in the kitchen and hallways, such as gas wall heaters) together with loft insulation, all contribute to making the home a warm and comfortable place. One government experiment some years ago tried sealing off the upstairs of a large house, and laying insulation on the upstairs floor, for an older person who no longer used the whole house. Well-fitted doors, and double doors to the outside, help to keep the house warm. Finding the money or persuading landlords to make heating improvements or alterations may not be easy. Practical measures that we can take ourselves include curtains that are heavy or lined (and drawing them closed before it gets dark) and using stuffed 'sausage dogs' at the base of doors to keep out draughts. Other simple draught-proofing measures may be helpful.

Safety is also important. Gas and Electricity Boards offer regular checks, usually free of charge to older people. Regular checks on gas fires are particularly necessary. Paraffin heaters can be dangerous and are best avoided if at all possible.

Some people prefer not to heat their bedrooms and sleep with the windows wide open, even in the middle of winter. But there is nothing particularly healthy about allowing one's body to get too cold while undressing and dressing or during the night. A gas wall heater on the landing and an electric blanket are useful compromises, although it is still preferable to use some form of heating in the bedroom itself. For those with central heating, it is, of course, easier to do this, as a radiator in the bedroom can be turned on for a short while before bedtime.

Adapting the home by installing a stairlift, a downstairs toilet, or a walk-in shower to avoid the problem of climbing in and out of the bath, are measures that remove risks and the worries that go hand in hand with them. But independence is also about the freedom to take the risks of everyday living. Frequent visits from a social worker, health visitor or a warden, or the recommendation to move to sheltered accommodation, are often the professional response to these risks. There is always an uproar in the newspaper when an elderly person who lives alone is found on the floor of his or her home following a fall. However, we may be much happier and more fulfilled if allowed to choose those risks we wish to take. I know one 90 year-old lady who risks life and limb to climb the steep slope behind her single-storey home to tend the garden and tackle the weeds. She is happy as long as she can continue to look after her garden, using two garden forks to aid her balance. Her social worker (who doesn't know about this) would be horrified!

The answer is to achieve a balance. The problem lies in persuading professional workers such as doctors and social workers to accept this: many of us may need educating to understand that better housing can help us to remain independent without unnecessary risks.

Making it Happen

Thinking about the best and most suitable housing, and planning the ideal home in our heads, is one thing. But how do we make the dream become reality?

The first thing to be considered is advice. It is important to make a careful decision if you are considering moving house, or to act promptly if you are worried about a broken gutter or a patch of damp on the wall; or anxious about keeping the house warm enough through the winter. Relatives and friends often offer their own brand of advice and, although this is useful, many problems to do with housing really need professional help. But where to go for that advice?

A lot will depend on where you live. A list of useful organisations and addresses is given in the Appendix. These may help if you have difficulty getting advice locally. But there are many avenues you can try first.

Let us start with general housing advice. Your local council may run a housing advice or housing aid centre. The local branch of the Citizens' Advice Bureau and Age Concern group may also be able to help. If there is any illness or disability making it difficult to manage at home or to get around, particularly if the toilet is up a flight of stairs, the place to go for help is the social services department of your local council. An occupational therapist (OT) is the most suitable person to advise you. In some areas an OT is referred to as an aids and adaptations officer. Their job is to help people to be as independent as possible; they know about the wide range of aids that are available to help with daily living, and about the sort of adaptations or alterations to your home that could be carried out to make it easier to manage. They can help to arrange a stairlift, for example, should the stairs become too difficult. Or they may suggest quite simple things, such as levers to make the taps easier to use.

If your social services department cannot offer any advice or help, then it would be worth taking the trouble to write to your local MP or councillor about it. This may not get you the help you need straight away, but will add one more voice to the lobby telling the Government that more community occupational therapists and other support services are badly needed.

Your doctor or health visitor may also be able to offer advice about your housing needs. Often they, too, are hard pressed, and as housing is not their direct concern it is something that they sometimes neglect. If more people asked their doctor questions such as: 'Is my illness going to lead to problems getting around the house?', 'Is my house warm enough in view of my medical condition?' and so on, perhaps more doctors would consider their patients' housing circumstances as well as the illness itself. One lady in her late 70s who was suffering from arthritis, said that her doctor had 'ordered' her to keep warm. He didn't know that her only toilet was outside and that the house was draughty.

Making Plans

It is never too early to start thinking about where to live in later life. When the children leave home may be the time to consider a move to a smaller house. Because of future anxiety about coping with repairs and maintenance, it might be sensible for home-owners to consider becoming tenants. Housing associations and local authorities are both worth approaching. Some local authorities unfortunately give low priority to rehousing home owners. In other areas, however, the council or housing association may offer to buy your house. You get a smaller home to rent, and at the same time a family will benefit by being able to rent your previous home from the council or housing association. A similar idea is for the council or housing association to buy your house while you remain living in it, thus becoming a tenant in your own home. If the house is too big the council or housing association could also offer to convert it into flats, with your agreement, and in this case, you would become a tenant of a part of your house, while another tenant occupied the rest.

These arrangements may become more widely available in the future, and it is always worth inquiring about what your particular local council or local housing associations have to offer. Don't be afraid to make suggestions if they offer very little!

Private tenants may find it easier to be rehoused by the local council or housing association. This is partly because some of the houses rented from private landlords are in such bad condition that private tenants may get a higher priority. Find out about local housing associations from the housing department of your local council.

It is sometimes too easy, however, to think that a move is necessary when something to do with your home presents a problem. For tenants it may be difficult to convince a landlord that the house needs repairs or improvements, or that the heating should be brought up to an adequate standard, or alterations carried out to make it easier to live there. This is when you need someone on your side. A housing aid or welfare rights centre will help to make sure that your landlord fulfills his responsibilities under the law. The social services department should offer help with any adaptations that are needed, and they may also be able to contribute to the cost. If, for example, you can no longer use your toilet because it is upstairs and the stairs are becoming very difficult to manage, you are entitled to a grant to cover all or most of the cost of installing a stairlift or a downstairs toilet. Walk-in showers, extra stair-rails and ramps are other items for which grant help is available. You could start by getting in touch with your local housing department, or asking a local councillor to help you.

Home owners are better placed to secure alterations or improvements, particularly now that building societies make mortgage funds freely available to pensioners for this purpose. There may be improvement grant aid available from your local council to help instal necessary amenities or to carry out major repairs and improvements. Different grants cover different types of work. Contact the Improvement Grant department of your local council for advice (or it may be the Environmental Health department that deals with these grants). Ask them to send you the free leaflet produced by the Department of the Environment on improvement grants. In some areas of the country there are schemes (details in the Appendix) to assist with organising the building work and with arranging the money – grant and mortgage – to pay for it. Failing that, there are some useful booklets, also listed in the Appendix, which describe the steps to take when organising building work yourself. There are also schemes in some areas, called 'Neighbourhood Energy Action', which can help to insulate and draught-proof your home and sometimes advise you on your heating. There is an address in the Appendix which you can contact. They will also help you to take advantage of the loft insulation grants which local authorities can give.

The new type of mortgage available from building societies for repairs and improvement work for older owners is particularly welcome. You pay back the amount borrowed from the proceeds of your house when it is eventually sold or inherited, and in the meantime you repay the interest only – hence, it is known as an interest-only mortgage or maturity loan. These are also sometimes available from local authorities. You can include any professional survey or solicitor's fees in the loan and, if you qualify for supplementary benefit or have limited savings, you may be able to have the interest met by an increase in your benefit. Under the supplementary benefit scheme you may also qualify for occasional financial help to cover more limited house repairs or redecoration. Organising the work and finding a builder can pose problems. Some areas have projects – sometimes called 'Staying Put' or 'Care and Repair', which will make the arrangements for you. If you are considering fairly extensive work or repairs and there is no such project in your area, it is worth employing an architect or surveyor to make the arrangements, and supervise and check the building work. A building surveyor is fine if there are few alterations and the work is mainly repairs, but it is advisable to approach an architect if any plans are required for alterations or improvements. The average fee to expect for this service is 10 per cent of the building work costs, and this usually represents value for money. Make sure you get a reputable surveyor or architect. The local authority or appropriate professional body should be able to recommend someone (see addresses in the Appendix). The fees can be met by the council improvement grant if you qualify for that, or alternatively can be included in the mortgage.

If you are contemplating building work, think about the little 'extras' that could be included while the builders are in. Make the most of the opportunity. A second stair-rail or raised electric power points are worth considering, particularly if you are already taking out an interest-only mortgage. A rail by the outside path or steps, a waist-level letterbox and cage, and a raised concrete ledge for the milk, are other ideas. Think about the kitchen: can you reach everything without having to climb on a stool? Could cupboards be better placed to make life easier?

There are some national organisations of reputable builders you could approach to find a contractor in your area. The local council may keep a list of builders it recommends. Try and find out about the builder you use before employing him.

If your home or the area you live in is really not suitable or to your liking, a move may be the answer. Ask yourself the following questions: do you have friends and neighbours living near your present home whom you depend on in any way – physically or socially? Would you be able or want to manage without them? Do you have a doctor, health visitor or home help whom you might miss? How easy would it be to make new friends? Who does your shopping when you are unwell? If you are considering a totally new area, how much do you know about it? If it is by the sea, find out what it is like in winter. It may not be quite the same place as it is in August. Check the rates in a different area. Is it going to be cheaper? Consider nearness to shops and bus routes and the layout of hills and slopes. Asking questions in this way may make you realise the advantages of your present house that have been taken for granted over many years. For council tenants who wish to move, there are two schemes which may help – the Tenants' Exchange Scheme and the National Mobility Office – the addresses are listed in the Appendix. The housing department of your local council should be able to give you the names and addresses of local housing associations to see what accommodation they might be able to provide, and an Age Concern fact sheet is available to explain more about housing associations.

Moving in with relatives may also not work out as intended. Will you be paying rent? Will you be able to consider a part of the house your own? Will you share all your meals (and the preparation and costs)? Will you be happy to become a resident babysitter or ironer? Make sure you discuss all the practical arrangements thoroughly before you come to a decision.

One other facility is available to those who own their own homes. This is a home income plan or mortgage annuity. It is a scheme which allows you to take out a mortgage which is then used to provide a regular income. This uses the mortgage to purchase an annuity from an insurance company, with the interest on the mortgage paid out of the annuity before your monthly payment is released. If you do not qualify for supplementary benefit (which, of course, you might lose if you did take out an annuity) it may be an option worth considering. A small part of the annuity (usually 10 per cent) can be taken as a lump sum at the beginning, and this can provide the necessary funds for any outstanding repairs or, for example, for installing central heating. It is best to ask a solicitor for advice about these schemes as it is extremely important to have independent advice about home income plans. An Age Concern fact sheet is also available.

In housing it is always necessary to plan ahead. By doing so, our homes should remain places which help us to lead independent and comfortable lives. It is to be hoped that, in the future, local councils and central government will allocate more funds to help meet the housing needs of elderly people. More housing advice centres, with advisors who can visit us in our own homes, more schemes to help make arrangements for repairs, improvements, heating installations and adaptations, and more choice in the different housing options available, would mean more satisfactory homes for a greater proportion of older people in this country.

6 Old People – New Lives: Residential Care

By Li McDerment

Attitudes to Old Age Homes – from poor house to a right to independent but supported living.

One Monday morning Mrs Brown was admitted to an establishment for elderly people from her rather isolated home in one of the Home Counties. She had spent several periods in hospital because of falls and other health problems, and had started to feel confused and disoriented at times. Her self-confidence and belief in her own ability to care for herself were on the wane and she had really wanted to stay on in the safety of the hospital. Her son, a solicitor who lived far away, became very worried and contacted the Social Services Department in the area where she lived. He was adamant that his mother had to be found a place in an old people's home.

At an emergency conference attended by representatives from the Social Services Department, Mrs Brown's GP and the son, but not Mrs Brown, it was decided to admit Mrs Brown for a two-week assessment period. The decision was a reluctant one. Mrs Brown did not want to go into an old people's home, the son insisted, for reasons too complex to explore here, and the professionals were divided in their opinion as to the suitable care provisions for the client. On the one hand, Mrs Brown was 'young' by the standards for people in residential homes, she was 75 years old and did not seem happy with the prospect of a period in 'a home'. On the other hand, there were risks involved in her remaining in her own home, which had become difficult to manage as she became less mobile. There was, above all, a chronic shortage of places in the county's few residential establishments for old people, and no vacancies in the sheltered housing schemes.

After two and a half weeks Mrs Brown returned home. Domiciliary services, such as they had become due to economic cuts, were mobilised. The crisis over, professionals and family alike had come to realise that 'home is always best', and were trying to encourage Mrs Brown to share their assumption. Six days later Mrs Brown committed suicide by taking a very large dose of her prescribed sleeping pills. The incident and her tragic death may be an indictment of social service practice. It more fundamentally reflects the attitude to old people's homes held by the community, including many professionals in the field.

Catalogues of disadvantages of residential care are all too common; often compiled by academics whose experience of communal living is remarkable chiefly for its brevity, these writings are usually referred to as the 'literature of dysfunction'. Lists of advantages, by contrast, are as rare as air on the top of Mount Everest and about as invigorating.[1]

There are problems in residential living and unhappy people in homes for the elderly. It is a fallacy, however, to believe that it is better for all people at all times to remain in the community. This way of thinking is supported by an idealisation of home life and independent living in old age, the 'myth of the golden years',[2] and an exaggerated belief in the availability, efficiency and usefulness of domiciliary services. The stereotype of 'the golden years' is contrasted with the traditional view that an old people's home is the equivalent to, or a continuation of, the workhouse and the idea that entering residential care is tantamount to social death and an admission of inadequacy, failure and a lack of worth.

The ideal life at home, well cared for, loved and supported, is juxtaposed to the evil institution, run for the benefit of the staff, where old folk sit along the walls in silence and where matron's word is the absolute rule. There are institutions which fit this description. There are also vast numbers of old people living in their own homes who, like Mrs Brown, are afraid of every new day and their ability to cope, who dislike the meals on wheels brought to them maybe in a hurry or by a harassed volunteer, who are cold, depressed and isolated: elderly people who might feel safe, cherished, involved and in good company in the unique setting of a home for elderly residents, offering good physical care as well as attention to emotional needs and social activities.

Good physical care lies at the heart of all residential provision. The distinguishing feature of residential care, as opposed to community provisions, is the focus on physical care. There is considerable evidence to suggest that material conditions and physical care provisions in residential establishments far exceed those in many an independent home; it is the area of discretion and choice from the residents' point of view that is lacking, not the quality of material provisions.

A Glasgow study, comparing the conditions of elderly people living in the community with those in hospital and residential care, pointedly refers to 'the survival of the unfittest', that is, those lucky enough to be admitted to residential care for medical and social reasons.

Even in the bad old days of the workhouse, physical conditions for the inmates were often better than they could aspire to outside the institution, despite the policy and clear intention that conditions should be so geared as to deter people from wanting to enter.[3]

The material standard and the degree of attention paid to physical care in homes for the elderly are, in fact, repeatedly criticised in the belief that these have been emphasised to the detriment of emotional needs and care. One can argue that it is in the satisfaction of the basic human needs, the environment, food, warmth, clothing, etc., that the philosophy and quality of the residential establishments are demonstrated. The essence (and skill) in providing residential care is to respond to emotional needs through sensitive physical care.

The problems of acceptability of old people's homes are compounded because of the uncertainty about their purpose. What should they be? How should care be provided? Are they 'hotels for pensioners', as Aneurin Bevan once dreamed? Are they to be regarded as housing units, or therapeutic establishments providing infinitely more than mere housing?

International comparisons seem to indicate that the housing and service flat model is emerging strongly in Scandinavia and Germany, while in Anglo-Saxon countries more emphasis is given to the therapeutic and social aspects of residential provisions for elderly people.[4]

The 1981 White Paper, *Growing Older*, provides some guidelines for residential care, but these are rather general. There is substantial evidence that the personality, training and background of the head of the home will largely influence the type of home provided and the way it is run, including the life style, daily living content and management of the establishment – staff included.[5]

Women Caring for Women

Around 95 per cent of elderly people live in the community and, although studies vary slightly in their estimates, it seems likely that between four and five per cent of the old are found in some form of institutional care – hospital, local authority, private or voluntary run establishment.[6]

Previously, one entered residential care in one's sixties. Today the average age is rapidly approaching 82. This reflects changing attitudes to residential care among the public and those professionally concerned, and an expansion of local authority and voluntary social service provisions.

It may also reflect a great deal of hidden suffering, with the elderly person caught between the lack of supportive community and family resources and the evil institution trap.

An estimated 131,000 elderly people are accommodated in local authority homes for elderly citizens or supported by the local authority in homes run by private or voluntary organisations.[7]

Private and voluntary organisations such as the Church, charitable and friendly societies and trades unions have a long history of providing for the old. Some organisations provide for certain groups, such as former employees or members. This may be an area to expand in the coming decades. At present, 70,000 places are provided in this way. The quality of the provisions varies. Some of the worst and some of the best aspects of practice are found in the voluntary sector.

The number of people who make a residential establishment their home has increased by about 20 per cent over the past decade.[8]

The need for supportive services for the old in the population will increase dramatically. In the coming 20 years, the number of people aged 60 and over will increase worldwide by 90 per cent.[9] In Britain, the number of people aged 65 and older has risen by as much as a third. This group now represents 15 per cent of the population. These changes will lead to considerable shifts in the age structure of the population. Life expectancy is increasing. By the end of the century, the group aged 75 and over is expected to increase by one-fifth, while the section of the population over 85 will increase by one-half.[10]

The distinguishing demographic characteristic of the older population group in the coming 25 years will thus be the 'new class of the very old'. In the same way that the concepts of child and teenager developed in response to social needs and conditions, a distinction between 'old' and 'very old' is now emerging. The French refer to the *troisième* and the *quatrième* age, the Scandinavians to 'pensioners' and 'very old citizens'.

An increasing proportion of women among the elderly in the population is found in most western countries. Life expectancy figures, as well as the sex ratio, indicate that this development is likely to persist and even increase.[11]

Three quarters of the elderly over 85 are women. Most care takers and care givers are women and many who look after aged relatives are themselves old.

We thus have a situation of women caring for women. Women's caring role has been emphasised and supported by political action through the ages; brought up to care for others, and often trapped by this in later life; taken for granted and maintained by a variety of social and economic measures. One can only speculate about the cost to society should women reject the caring, nurturing role designed for them. Little wonder that community care often reads women-care, and is based on economic considerations rather than the needs of the women themselves.

The idea of women caring for women holds equally true for homes for the old. Most residents are female, the staff predominantly of the same gender. What are the implications of a 'community of women', designed by social and economic forces rather than by choice? Women are often less assertive, have more problems in saying 'no' and are more influenced by public opinion and social feedback from the group around them.[12] When trying to understand life and social processes in an old people's home, we need to consider relationships to authority, the success or failure of residents' committees, attempts to change power structures and communication patterns in residential communities. These are certainly influenced by women, particularly women born at the beginning of this century, finding self-assertion exceedingly difficult and political roles alien.

Care staff often report that they have higher expectations of women residents, both with regard to cleanliness, ability for self care and coping with household chores. Conflict with women residents over bed making is thus often reported in training groups and seminars. The effect of the carer's own relationship with the women in her life – her mother, daughter, etc. – on her ability to provide sensitive and often intimate physical and emotional care for elderly women, is a largely unexplored area. When approached in a training context, the carers often react with surprise: 'I never thought of that,' or consternation: 'I cannot see the relevance.'

Care staff may treat elderly people as if they were children. A care assistant once told me that there was little difference between her four year-old and the resident she was working with. This is, in part, a protective mechanism, designed to keep uncomfortable feelings and thoughts at bay, such as one's reaction to other women becoming more and more dependent on one's ability to be caring and giving, on one's stronger body and maybe faster working mind.

Caring work is stressful, whether in one's own home or in a residential establishment. The combination of high staff or care giver stress, high dependency needs on the side of the old person and power and authority invested in the care giver, may be a sure formula for abuse, be it so-called 'granny bashing' in the home of a close relative, or the forms of abuse which could go undiscovered in residential homes. The need for effective monitoring systems and training goes without saying.

Reasons for Being in Residential Care

There seem to be easily identifiable reasons for elderly people seeking admission to a residential home. The main ones are disability and inability to look after oneself, or anticipated future problems, together with inadequate housing.[13] Admission often follows illness or the death of a family member who provided care. Family stress and loneliness account for less than 10 per cent of the admissions.

A DHSS survey[14] points to an increase in emergency

admissions, accounting for about half of all admissions. It is debatable whether this reflects a reluctance to plan for admission to an old age home or lack of resources. When resources are scarce, it is difficult to find places for people other than in an emergency, or if their need is very obvious.

Whatever the reason, the speed with which many old people are transferred to residential care can be harmful to their health, making it difficult to adapt to new surroundings and gain a sense of well-being in their new home.

It is dangerous to generalise about the elderly; older people do, however, tend to be slower and need a longer process of preparation for change, eg. more opportunities for discussion and information. Although the pressure for physical comfort and safety in the form of shelter, food and warmth may be great at the time, the skill lies in supporting and protecting the elderly person while making the decision.

Developments and Important Changes

Although homes for the elderly are not getting a larger share of economic or human resources, the ways in which people are cared for are being carefully looked at.

Today's old age homes are smaller, purpose-built units, housing perhaps 50 people. There is a trend towards small group living. A typical old age home may consist of four self-contained flatlets for about six to eight people, who share a communal dining room and lounge, bathrooms and toilets. Each resident has or shares a bedroom. This type of unit allows people maximum participation and control over their lives and reduces the number of people the old person has to relate to, thus taking away some of the difficulties of communal living. The continuity of care staff is considered to be of great importance.

This is further demonstrated by the idea of the 'key worker'. Under this system of working, each staff member is responsible for the physical and emotional well-being of a small group of, let us say, five residents. If help is necessary with bathing, clothes purchases, contact with relatives, etc., the resident knows who to call on for help. Present staffing ratios and structure make 'key working' in its ideal form difficult to attain.

Major changes are occurring in the training and selection of staff. A very small proportion of staff in homes for the elderly hold an appropriate qualification. Those qualified are mainly nursing trained. There is, however, a tendency towards social service and social work training, particularly for management staff. This trend reflects a change; 'support' rather than 'nursing' is what is often needed, although this is not always the case and nursing qualifications may still dominate in the private sector. Attention is also being given to the training and selection of basic care staff. These are at present classified as manual workers with low pay and poor career prospects. Improvements in this area are the most urgent of all.

In many establishments, residents are encouraged to take an active part in the management and running of the unit through resident committees, use of contracts to regulate staff/resident relations, and resident/staff meetings.

A visitor to an old age home will often find a range of individual and group activities, including a resident-run bar. This is in response to a growing awareness that purposeful social activity is not only the spice of life but essential for survival and that, for example, senile behaviour is, in part, social in nature and can be, if not cured, contained and prevented by social means.

Senile dementia and incontinence pose problems to those who live and work in homes for the elderly. Expertise in the treatment and management of these aspects of old age is generally lacking, having been given low priority in research and clinical study.

There is, however, reason for some optimism. First of all, the problem is being acknowledged and gaining recognition as a worthwhile area for study and research; secondly, training in these areas is being intensified; and, thirdly, on the practice side, staff concerned with the daily management of these problems are encouraged to record and in different ways make better use of the accumulation of day-to-day experience of working with the mentally frail and/or incontinent person. It is increasingly common for residential establishments to offer day care facilities for people living in the neighbouring community, short term care to relieve the permanent care giver, regular respite care (also designed to provide support for the family caring for elderly relatives, or to elderly people themselves by providing the opportunity for regular periods in a sheltered environment), and rehabilitation for people who, after long periods of hospitalisation, wish to return home but need a period of assessment and rejuvenation of old skills. Whenever possible these services are used to help a prospective resident in deciding whether to enter the old age home.

Services for the elderly can be thought of as a 'continuum of care'. This assumes an increasing need for social and supportive services for the old person. An elderly person might first need help from volunteers and brief contacts with the social or health services; later, need for domiciliary services may develop, later still, the need for day care, sheltered housing and finally residential care. Hospital care may be the ultimate stage. It is envisaged that an old person could move between different parts of the continuum according to need; for instance, back and forth between domiciliary and day care services.

Entering Residential Care

The decision to make a residential establishment one's home is a far-reaching and riskful one.

The move should not be undertaken without a proper assessment of the needs of the old person and the risks involved in remaining at home; it should be of obvious benefit and properly prepared for. This can be helped by the family and the social worker. Relatives may shy away from discussing openly the reasons for wanting a mother, aunt or father-in-law to enter a residential home and may need information and sensitive guidance and support. The sense of rejection and guilt can be overwhelming.

Increasingly, staff from the residential home visit the prospective resident at home or in hospital and, if at all possible, the elderly person pays a visit to the home or comes for a trial stay.

Good practice requires that the elderly person is fully involved in the decision to enter an old persons' home; this includes a full exploration of the alternatives, expectations and reasons for the change. It is taxing, but possible, to involve even the person who appears to have lost touch with reality in this decision.

Part of the preparation must focus on practical arrangements about such matters as the disposal of the existing home; although each decision will have to be taken individually, the general rule would be to maintain property and possessions for the settling in period. This aids the transition and gives the old person a sense of security, providing she/he is convinced that assistance will be forthcoming in sorting out tenancy, bills and the range of practical matters which are bothersome at the best of times. Reassurance of practical help is particularly important in emergency admissions. In these circumstances it is essential that the new resident, as well as the relatives, has the opportunity to discuss feelings of confusion, loss, fear and rejection.

It is often the obvious that is overlooked. When an elderly man or woman is entering residential care from hospital or another establishment, one must ensure that spectacles, dentures, other aids and medication are included among personal belongings.

Residential workers often report that professionals and relatives involved in the admission to the home leave the old person with unrealistic expectations of what life will be like. The resident who enters communal living expecting 'support and help' in daily living will most likely maintain her/his independence and mobility longer than the person who has been 'sold' the idea of hotel comfort and total care. There are many risks in providing total care: it encourages institutionalisation and a high degree of dependency, narrows choice for the resident, reduces the sources of dignity that go with self-care, and minimises a person's means of self-esteem and value.

Dependency and institutionalisation are always a risk in residential care and homes must counteract these tendencies. They must emphasise independence, choice and power sharing, match the needs of the resident with the resources of the establishment and set realistic short- and long-term goals for the resident's stay.

Daily Life

What is daily life in a home like? It is becoming increasingly usual for residents to bring their furniture and personal belongings. Residents' rooms thus become individual and personal, far removed from our image of the evil institution. Rules and regulations vary, as do mealtimes and the quality of food. Many establishments experiment with flexible mealtimes, especially at breakfast, choice of menus and a minimum of rules; smoking in bed is likely to be a forbidden area, but pets may be welcome.

Each home should provide an information booklet setting out its aims and objectives, facilities offered, complaints procedure, etc. The information brochure from one establishment states that its aim is to make the resident feel at home, and to have things around her/him which bring pleasure. The booklet points out that none of the things the person enjoys needs to stop because she or he enters the home. Indeed, the author states '. . . with the help we can offer, you'll probably find that you can do lots more. Your life is still your own, and your friends and visitors are as free to come and go as you are. Visitors are welcome any time, any day.'[15]

A visitor to this particular home would, (if he had been invited to one of the units), see very old and handicapped people, living their lives. They might be setting about getting up, preparing breakfast or 'elevenses', chatting, reminiscing, relaxing, or reading the paper. People may be busy in their own bedrooms or setting off to wash some 'smalls' in the laundry. Someone might be going out for a breath of fresh air, down to the shops or out with a daughter; another might be awaiting a visitor. It might be a day when one or two are joining in the activities in the Day Centre, or it may be the day when all will be meeting to discuss what is happening in the group and to make some plans for the Carnival float, for a celebration party or for an outing. Sam might stroll in and out to the sunshine where his gleaming bicycle is propped up, ready for a spin as soon as he feels ready. The keen gardeners might be out working on their raised beds, or in the greenhouse. Several might be awaiting the arrival of their friend who has had a spell in hospital. There will be a 'welcome home' for her. It could be great stress for some who know that life is quietly drawing to a close for one of their group. Some will be ready to sit with her and to help in whatever way they can. Others might be very quiet, thinking . . .

For another group there could be tension in the air, with anger and annoyance near the surface over something said or done. Perhaps someone 'isn't speaking', which can be as difficult as if she were!

The visitor would notice above all the lack of staff bustle and the emphasis upon interaction, exchange and preoccuption. Activities which require negotiation, consultation and mutuality entirely change the old familiar picture of old people sitting around the edges of a large room whilst staff run to and fro.[16]

Residential life often involves a very old person in many new relationships. To be confronted with 50 new residents and maybe 30 staff can be devastating. A desire to withdraw, to isolate oneself, and a degree of depression are common ways of coping with the stress. These signs must be recognised for what they are and not be taken as expressions of the onset of dementia.

A residential home needs to be organised so as to minimise stress and promote a few, but important, caring relationships. The move towards small-group living and key working is thus encouraging.

The most difficult aspect of communal living may be the lack of privacy. A new resident may have to accept as part of everyday life, for example, eating in public when dribbling, having incontinence problems scrutinised by staff and other residents, and the need for help with intimate physical care. A great deal of sensitivity and empathy is required from the staff to provide assistance without intrusion. The attitude which prompts a staff member to stand in the door of the communal lounge and call out in a loud voice, 'Are you dry, Mrs C?' is hopefully becoming a thing of the past, as training and supervision improve.

Many residential establishments would like to view the relationship with the resident's relatives and friends as a partnership. A near relative may be encouraged to come in and help the resident with bathing, hair care, clothes purchases, etc. Experience and common sense show that it is easier for relatives to become involved in the home, if they are given a more purposeful role than the traditional 'bedside hospital visitor' one. Regular visits to the relative's home are also encouraged.

It is important to remember, however, that many residents may be isolated before they enter the home, others may have relatives and friends who are themselves very old. Social relationships may need to be provided within the home or with some creative thinking from the community.

The Residential Establishment and the Community

A residential home is part of the local community and must be recognised as such. Avenues are being explored to develop residential homes into resource centres for the community, offering their material and human resources in a wider context. Communal facilities should be opened up as community areas and made available to other groups or individuals not living in the home. One establishment, for example, shares the swimming pool with groups of mothers and toddlers and with groups from the local school for mentally handicapped children. Their bar has been converted into a social club now used by the community, and an advice and information service operates from the home.

There is considerable scope for imaginative and creative developments. The needs of the residents must, however, be considered first and foremost, and one aim of the resource centre is to benefit both residents and the community through a sharing of resources and expertise. Residents of the home referred to above sometimes complain of an 'invasion of kids', and sensitivity is needed to cope with these problems.

For some people, communal life can be absorbing, even though they are closed off from outside influences. For others, it can seem like 'social death'. Individual residents need encouragement and active support to maintain and develop contacts with the world outside. This may be achieved through help from staff to re-establish old friendships, or through schemes and projects which offer opportunities for residents to come into contact with groups from the neighbourhood. Two illustrations would be the re-introduction of a very old man into the British Legion and the further education project which used residents from one elderly persons' home to provide information and focus for a local history society.

Degree of Satisfaction in Homes for the Elderly

One important study found that a high proportion of residents in old age homes liked living there. In one area, the proportion of people claiming to like the home and their life style was as high as 90 per cent; in other areas it fell to two thirds and three quarters. Others said that they liked the place and the life style there with qualifications. 12 per cent were unhappy with life in the establishment. The main causes for their unhappiness appeared to be shared accommodation and the distance from family, relatives and friends.[17]

Social relationships are very important in determining how a resident adjusts to communal life. Mr A was 87 years old and often spoke about leaving the home and finding a flat outside: '. . . I did not like being in the home at first. It upset me to see so many people a lot more helpless than myself. This is a wonderful place and everything is done for them as humanely as possible. I often marvel how the matron performs her numerous tasks. Some are so helpless – the inmates I mean – that they ought to be in hospital. And some in my opinion, ought to be looked after by their families.'[18] Mr A's last comment is most telling and no doubt expresses his own sentiments. When another man was admitted for short-term care to give the family a break, the two men became friends. The newcomer eventually remained in the home and he and Mr A were always sitting together in a small lounge, pulling their families and other residents to pieces. Mr A began to feel more settled and rarely talked of moving out to a small flat. He started to make more contacts in the home. 'The right kind of opportunity to interact with a suitable other person made a great deal of difference to his ability to adjust to his past losses and his current environment.[19] Skilful staff can help create opportunities for residents to make new relationships. Residential work with the old gives the caring professions a chance to create an environment which allows the old and the very old to be treated as adults with fundamental rights to choice, privacy, respect and realistic help and assistance.

The very old are among the most vulnerable in our society. Precisely because of that, they need to be heard and we need to learn to listen. We must listen to what Mrs Brown has to say about her life and fears, and about her knowledge of ageing and dependency. We can ill afford to wait till we grow old. 'They'll know when they're old', is too often muttered in vain along the corridors of homes for the elderly.

A final statement from an elderly woman in one home makes this point clearly. 'Do you know what has been the nicest thing about living here – you have listened to me and allowed me to live until I die.'

To enter a residential home is a dramatic move. It can be very difficult to judge what type of home and environment will suit you, a near relative or client. Here are some brief pointers. Names and addresses of useful organisations follow in the Appendix at the end of the book.

1   Plan and prepare for the possibility of admission to residential care to avoid the stress of a crisis move.
2   Start with the premise that there is a choice of placement and viable alternatives.
3   Pursue an active involvement in the admission process;

select the 'right' place, visit, stay for a trial period.

4   Ask for and read the establishment information booklet and find out about resident involvement in the running of the home.

5   Consider cost and value for money.

6   Consider the building and how well it is adapted to suit people with impaired mobility. Are there handrails, ramps for wheelchairs, working lifts, aids for bathing, etc.?

7   How many single and double rooms are there? Will you have to share a room?

8   Do the rooms have handbasins? How many bathrooms are there?

9   Consider fabrics and furnishings – what do they tell you about the ethos of the home? Can your mother live with purple flock wallpaper?

10   What does the place smell like? Is there a distinct odour of urine?

11   Make sure you talk to the staff and test their attitudes to the home and the people who live there.

12   Find out about staffing ratio and training.

13   If a voluntary or private home, find out which local authority has registered and is inspecting the home.

14   Determine the complaints procedure and be suspicious if none exists in writing.

15   Ascertain whether the domestic routine, mealtimes, etc., serve the needs of the resident or the staff rota.

16   Find out how the person entering the establishment can maintain a certain degree of independence. Can she do her own washing and care for her room and belongings? What activities and facilities are on offer?

17   Have a meal in the home if possible. Do the residents enjoy their meal?

18   How are medical needs responded to? Can the residents keep their own GP?

19 When considering a private home, refer to the code of practice for residential establishments in the private and voluntary sector. It is available from the Centre for Policy on Ageing.

7 Coping with Death and Bereavement

By Ethel Holloway and Viveka Nyberg

For mine own part, I could be well content
To entertain the lag end of my life
With quiet hours.

> Shakespeare, *Henry IV, Part 1*

Worcester, in these words, expresses the wishes of people throughout the ages, for security and peace in the last decades of life, particularly as it begins to draw to its close. Like Worcester, however, who spoke these words on the eve of a battle in which his forces were to be defeated, modern man has his struggles and anxieties as he reaches the 'lag end of his life'. Dr Robert Butler wrote that, far from living out the final years serenely, 'the older person may be barraged by grief, loneliness, anxiety and a loss of self esteem.'[1] Each generation, perhaps, has its own particular battles to overcome. In this chapter we should like to compare present attitudes towards death and bereavement with the attitudes which existed when today's generation of elderly people was growing up, and to focus on the particular 'battles' which they have to face today; to discuss some ways by which anxieties can be lessened and to think about the spiritual and emotional dimensions. In the second part of the chapter we look at the importance of the mourning process, attempting to understand the elderly person's experience of loss.

Changing Attitudes

Unlike our Victorian grandparents, we look forward to

greater life expectancy, and to a considerably better standard of living than they did, as a result of the immense technological changes, particularly since the Second World War. The expectation of life, and the number of men and women living to the Biblical three-score-years-and-ten and beyond, has grown considerably since the beginning of the century, thanks to the decline of maternal and infant mortality, the conquest of the killer diseases of childhood and, following successive Public Health Acts, today's greatly improved environmental standards. While many people approaching retirement will have experienced the death of close friends and relatives, the younger generation may not come into contact with death in their personal lives until, perhaps, the death of a grandparent. At the same time we are continually bombarded by the media with the violent presence of death in murders and devastating acts of nature and man. Death was a much more familiar experience to families in all walks of life at the beginning of this century, and the religious and social observances around the mourning period enhanced the respect shown to the dead, and gave permission for the bereaved to mourn. The complicated rituals have almost disappeared. We no longer 'go into mourning', which graduated from the deepest black of 'widows' weeds' to pale mauve as the months passed. Blinds were drawn as a mark of respect, and nowadays it is rare to see men taking off their hats as a funeral cortège passes. Today's more clinical approach has contributed to the taboo which has grown up around death.

Retirement and redundancy are commonplace features of the period in which we live. A century ago, the average man went on working for as long as possible whether he wanted to or not, because there were few pension funds and there was work to be done. Retirement is a time of major change and emotional upheaval. Familiar signposts are torn down – the individual's role in society is swept away overnight, and new paths have to be sought. Retirement can offer opportunities to explore new interests, learn new skills, and to move into different social circles. For those who reach retirement unprepared for the changes which are to come, or for those who find change difficult to achieve, it may be a time of loneliness, devoid of all sense of purpose. This can lead to depression and to the development of attitudes which will, in turn, lead to a old age of boredom and regret, hankering after the past which will not return, fearful of the future. 'Where retirement is seen as an experience of loss, with grief and depression predominating, the person is ill-prepared to meet bereavement or his own death.'[2]

The other change which has taken place in the lifetime of those growing old today is the decline in western countries of religious faith, bringing with it doubts and disbeliefs about a life after death.

Fear of Dying

Psychiatrists tell us, and few of us would doubt them, that we all have irrational fears of death. Through adolescence and middle life, we prefer to 'assume that we are immortal, immune from the laws of celestial gravity.'[3] As we grow older, however, we become aware that we have not got all the time in the world. Retirement may be the time when we begin to reflect on our ultimate mortality, or the knowledge may impinge upon us when we become aware that we are ourselves the 'older generation' – those who came before us have all died. For many it will be the death of a life partner, or the death of a friend of long-standing with whom it was possible to share memories of childhood. This awareness is often the time for reflecting on the less tangible aspects of life – its meaning and purpose – and for coming to terms with the achievements and disappointments of our own lives. It may find expression in more practical details, such as making one's will and tidying one's affairs, or as Mary Stott, writing in her eighties, suggests, 'retrenching, discarding and shedding in a literal and physical sense.'[4]

A 95 year-old lady of our acquaintance who lived alone, and managed her own affairs with very little help from anyone else, once asked one of us to fetch her something from her wardrobe. It came as a shock to see the paucity of her clothing. There was enough for her needs but it was as if everything else had been packed away, and she was ready to leave at any moment. She was serene and peaceful, interested in what was happening around her, talking about her previous relationships, and had come to terms with earlier vicissitudes and disappointments.

Some Ways of Coping with Anxieties

In the *Nursing Times*, G. S. Perks suggests that one of the ways in which the thought of death may be made more acceptable is to consider how we would wish to die. Such an exercise would vary from culture to culture, and from age to age. For the older person, the wish is most likely to be for a peaceful death, pain-free, in familiar surroundings, supported by those who are nearest and dearest. It is knowing that this might not happen that causes concern and fear. The thought of a lonely old age, with increasing physical and mental frailty, incontinence, loss of memory, immobility and the fear of becoming a burden to families and to society can be a constant nagging anxiety, coupled with the fear of being admitted to unfamiliar institutional care. The indignities associated with this stereotyped picture of ageing, perhaps suggest that we should think again. A more realistic approach might be to die with dignity, with the individual, and those caring for him, accepting the infirmities which may be present as death approaches.

Fear of Pain

The Reverend Michael Gaine writes of several research projects which have been carried out among elderly people. In one project, the result had shown that most people questioned had denied a fear of death, but were afraid of the process of dying and of painful and protracted deaths. The hospice movement, now widely known largely through the pioneering work in this country of Dr Cicely Saunders, is helping to eradicate such fears by the work which is being done to control pain through the appropriate use of drugs, to enable patients 'to die free from pain and in serene awareness'. Medical care is linked with concern for the patient and his family's emotional, social and spiritual needs. David Hobman describes hospices as 'places where the dying of all ages can be helped to encounter what religions would describe and pray for in the terms of a happy death, surrounded by love, and often in the company of their family.'[5] The movement is now extending its care through its home nursing service. In a recent radio programme discussing the work of St Christopher's Hospice, an elderly woman patient, who died a few days after the programme had been made, said in a buoyant voice that, since she had been a patient at St Christopher's, she had been happier than at any other time of her life, and added, 'I feel more alive.' The fear of pain and of a prolonged and suffering existence is an argument for the right of the individual to be in control of his life through voluntary euthanasia. Dr Murray Parkes argues against this, suggesting that while such services as offered by the hospice movement (ideas which are being taken up and used in general hospitals and in general practice) are available, it would be tragic if euthanasia or assisted suicide were carried out instead of good medical care.

Talking about Feelings

The hospice movement was started primarily for the care of

patients suffering from terminal cancer; in an atmosphere of loving care, a patient is enabled to talk about his anxieties and to come to terms with his impending death. But it does not need a hospice environment for such confidence to be established, although in many families it is often difficult for feelings to be shared at a deep level if such a habit has not been cultivated over the years. Sensitive awareness of the meaning rather than the words can sometimes help to unlock the feelings of the elderly person. This may occur in a group situation where a person feels secure and supported. The work done with a group of elderly people in Montreal enabled them to release their negative feelings, to accept their past failures, to feel accepted by the group for what they were, and to feel in control of their own future, instead of slipping into a state of stagnation and a wish to die. The conspiracy of silence about death which we often encounter makes it difficult for an elderly person to put thoughts and feelings into words. It is helpful to be able to express these thoughts and anxieties, so that if possible, misunderstandings can be resolved, leading to a great awareness of the choices to be made. It can be painful for younger family members to accept such confidences. They do not wish to consider the possibility of death, and so by saying, 'Don't talk like that, Gran,' effectively block out the possibility of further discussion of such feelings. Encouraging discussion, however, may help the old person to develop a sense of personal fulfilment: 'If only we'd talked about it,' is often the cry of the widowed spouse who is left to cope alone, when the partner who has died was the one on whom the other relied.

Mrs A, who was helped by a volunteer from the Wandsworth Bereavement Support Group, had always been the ailing one of the partnership; 'the creaking gate', she called herself. She and her husband had assumed that she would be the first to die, and he had always told her that when this happened he would be quite willing to go into a residential home. When he died suddenly while they were on holiday, she felt utterly rejected and powerless to carry on alone. She had relied on him in every way, and life without him seemed intolerable and hopeless.

The Montreal group discovered that worries about the future decreased when they were put into words. Discussion and knowledge of the practical issues of everyday living can be of great help to the surviving partner.

The Spiritual Dimension
From Man's earliest days, the great religions of the world have taught that there is a life after death, although none know with certainty the form of this spiritual existence. Christians believe that, through his death on the Cross, Christ overcame death and opened the gates of everlasting life to all who follow God's commandments. Christ told his disciples, 'In my Father's house are many mansions.'[6]
Scepticism and doubt are not peculiar to the present century, but in today's world, with its materialistic outlook and its 'high tech' components, there has been a decline in matters of the spirit and a denial by many of an afterlife. Relatively few people believe in Heaven or Hell in a literal or Biblical sense but, according to D. B. Bromley, a large number have a belief in some kind of personal existence after death. For each of us, such beliefs are very personal and relate to our own life experiences. Murray Parkes suggests that the meaning of a life beyond life must arise from our faith in life itself. Erikson feels that the eighth and final stage of a person's development is the achievement of an integrated state of mind – the acceptance of an order and meaning in the totality of one's life, past, present and future. Despair represents the fear that life is too short to make up the deficits of past life and

suggests a fear of death. Maturity does not dwell on things past, but is a continuing experience involving the present and the future. Olave, Lady Baden-Powell, wanted on her death 'no mourning as such – all rejoicing and happy remembrances and delight at my having completed my life's work. My prayer has been answered – God give me work till the end of my life, God give me life till my work is done'.

In a very different setting, Miss B at 90 was getting used to life in a residential home. Her life-long friend, with whom she had shared her home, had died, her own health was deteriorating and she was no longer able to look after herself. Her independent spirit had helped her to manage on her own for as long as possible, but she was eventually obliged to give up and sell her home. Life in a residential setting was very different from anything she had experienced before, and she used to talk about the idiosyncracies of her fellow residents with understanding and compassion. When she wished me a 'Happy New Year', she added 'I love the New Year, you never know what's around the corner.' She had come to terms with the past, with its share of happiness and sadness, accepted the present and looked ahead to the future, whatever it was to be.

The Mourning Process
The way each of us approaches the experience of grief and sorrow is highly individual. It may depend on personality, previous life experience and how we have dealt with other crises in our lives.

It is also influenced by the nature of the relationship we have had with the dead person and what he or she meant to us. Nevertheless, some features can be observed in nearly every bereavement, whatever the age of the bereaved person, which justifies us regarding grief as a distinct psychological process. This can be divided into four phases. In our outline of these phases we will follow Dr Murray Parkes' description, from his book *Bereavement – Studies of grief in adult life*. In the first phase of mourning we tend to feel shock and disbelief. It may last from a few moments to several days. There is a feeling that what has happened cannot be true. The bereaved person is in a sense trying to deny the loss.

This merges gradually into the next phase as the shocked person begins to acknowledge that the loved one has died. The shock and disbelief give way to the full impact of grief. This second phase is characterised by pining and searching for the dead person. Pining is a strong desire for the person who is gone, a preoccupation with wishing he or she were here. It is also a search for the person who has been lost. Both Parkes and Bowlby maintain that human beings have an urge similar to certain animals, to search for what has been lost. This is apparent in children who have been separated from their parents, in particular from their mothers. For children there is, of course, survival value in this kind of behaviour because if they search and cry for the lost parent she is more likely to be recovered. Although adult human beings know that this is not so, it does not stop them from searching. The search may even be conscious or deliberate: 'I can't help looking for him everywhere', 'I walk around the streets searching for him.' Even bereaved people who do not actively search will often recognize this as an impulse. For many people the search for things which stimulate a memory of the dead person may give consolation. The bereaved person may recognise this kind of searching as irrational, and for some it can be quite frightening, since it may be experienced as a fragmentation bordering on mental illness. It is usually reassuring to be told that this is a natural and commonplace experience shared by many bereaved people. Searching gradually becomes less frequent as time passes, although the urge to search may reappear at times when the loved one is sorely missed, for example around the time of anniversaries.

Anger is another distinct feeling which plays a part in bereavement. It is difficult to recognise this for what it is. We are angry as well as sad when we lose someone important to us. For example, the anger may be turned against the hospital, the doctor or against someone who is trying to help. The bereaved person may turn the anger inwards and will blame himself or herself, and it is usually relatively easy to find opportunities to feel at fault. For example, what was done or not done prior to the death can be used as an excuse. There is usually no real reason for these feelings of self-blame and guilt. Often the only relief we can offer the bereaved is the re-assurance that they have done all they possibly could have done.

As time passes and if all goes well, the episodes of yearning and searching become less frequent and the feelings of acute sadness become less intense. Instead, the bereaved person is faced with long periods of aimlessness and apathy which characterise the third phase of loss. At this point there are often strong feelings of depression and also a sense of 'giving-up': the giving-up of objects and experiences which had previously been shared with the loved one. Attitudes have to change and the bereaved person is struggling with accepting a new life style. It is during this period that the most active part of the mourning process takes place. At this stage support and a sympathetic listening ear from a friend or a professional person can be invaluable. The intense emotions which are experienced as overwhelming and frightening may become more bearable if they can be expressed and contained. It is now that the bereaved person is trying to sort out what has been lost. It is not a matter of leaving behind all the clutter and detail of the relationship; rather it is a process of finding out what has gone and must be left buried with the past and what can be carried over into the future. New assumptions have to be made about the world and new skills have to be learned. Slowly and gradually, most people begin to regain a sense of the future. The existence of children and grandchildren help to sustain the feeling that life goes on. There is often a marked change around the time of the first anniversary of the death. This becomes a natural point for reflection and review, because a full circle has been passed – wedding anniversaries, birthdays, Christmas, holidays, etc. To have survived all these during the course of the first year may give strength and courage.

There is also a fourth phase of the mourning process which can be described as reorganisation. In a sense this phase never ends, as life will continue to be reorganised. Obviously reorganisation becomes more difficult with advancing years and is easier for people healthy enough to be able to live a more active and fulfilling life. The presence of grandchildren, hobbies, friends and, above all, internal strength and resources, influence the kind of adjustment the bereaved person will eventually make.

The Very Elderly

We know very little about the particular needs of elderly bereaved people, but it seems that their response to bereavement is different from that of younger age groups. The feelings of acute grief appear to be less intense although feelings of loss last for a very long time.

Many people believe that very old people, because they experience bereavement more frequently, somehow become 'immune' to the loss of relatives and friends. In fact, the reverse may be closer to reality. For example, the largest proportional rise in suicides has been among the over 75 year-olds. With advancing years, any change becomes more difficult and the task of reorganising life after such a major crisis may be impossible, physically or mentally.

The death of a son or daughter is a tragedy for parents of any age and for an old parent to lose an adult son or daughter may be an experience from which they will never recover. It is emotionally difficult to come to terms with the feelings of unfairness and illogicality which are often strongly experienced when a child dies first. In addition, the old parent may feel pushed aside and rejected when the widow or widower is seen and treated as the chief mourner.

Atypical grief

Individual experiences of bereavement are all different, although it is usually considered atypical not to mourn at all. For many different reasons, the bereaved person may be unable to mourn and will put on a 'brave face' and continue as if nothing has changed. The mourning process will then become delayed and prolonged or it will be intensified when the grief finally breaks through. When people try hard to avoid mourning it does eventually catch up. It may take a long time, sometimes years, before a further crisis such as another bereavement becomes a breaking point. On the other hand, if a bereaved person is still acutely and persistently grieving beyond the first year there is also cause for concern. Because mourning is not only an emotional reaction to death but is also seen as a 'duty' to the dead, some people will be reluctant to come to the final phase of the mourning process. They may need to be told that they have done their duty and be given permission to stop grieving, just as others may need permission to express their grief in the first place. However if the grief reaction develops into deep depression or suicidal feelings, help may be needed from a psychiatrist or an experienced bereavement counsellor.

Other Losses

It is not only through the deaths of loved ones that we experience loss. Other major losses may follow a grief pattern similar to that of the mourning process. The amputation of a limb or the experience of moving house can produce similar psychological reactions. It may appear far-fetched to compare the loss of a husband with the loss of a leg. Nevertheless, the amputee goes through a process of mourning in which he or she moves from denial of the amputation towards acceptance. There are typical grief manifestations like loss of appetite and weight, sleeping disturbances, pining for lost activities such as swimming and walking. Feelings of anger and bitterness may arise as well as difficulties in adjusting to a new way of life. Other crises which involve considerable loss are retirement from work or entering an old people's home. The latter case means loss of independence and there may be a long period of mourning and pining for the old home, particularly if the move was involuntary. It is important for staff and relatives to understand this, so that they can accept this process without feeling rejected by an apparent lack of gratitude.

How Can We Help

Recently bereaved people will sometimes tell of a friend or neighbour who crosses the road to avoid them rather than offer the customary greeting or sympathy. Naturally this is very upsetting for the bereaved person, since it confirms the feelings of utter rejection and of being stigmatised. This kind of behaviour suggests how difficult it is to face death and loss as an integral part of living. E. Kübler-Ross observes that the people best able to help with bereavement are those who have come to terms with their own fears of death. This may sound abstract and theoretical, yet it can be translated into practical language by thinking of the helper as somebody who can listen with quiet sympathy, unafraid of the overwhelming feelings which may be expressed by the bereaved person.

Bereaved people need the opportunity to talk about their grief and the death, sometimes over and over again, and to express their feelings of sadness, anger, guilt and resentment. It is helpful to feel that these experiences are accepted as reasonable and normal under the circumstances.

Perhaps the most difficult aspect for someone close to a recently bereaved person is the fact that there may be very little he or she can do or say to make things better. The clock cannot be turned back and the dead person cannot be brought to life again. It is important that the bereaved person feels wanted and cared for, although sometimes there is little we can do but be silent and listen. During the initial stage of grief the bereaved person may appear very unappreciative of the help offered, at times even rejecting it. It is often not until the acute impact has lessened that he or she is able to appreciate the support and encouragement offered by friends and relatives. Although it can be hard to see somebody close to us distraught and unhappy, a turning point does come for most people when they feel capable of taking up the threads of life again. For those who have been helping it is rewarding to see that somebody who has suffered so much grief and sorrow can emerge stronger and with renewed zest for life.

Appendices

USEFUL ADDRESSES

1 Changing Relationships
Campaign for Homosexual Equality (CHE), 274 Upper Street, London N1.

2 Adding Spice to Life: Leisure
Age Concern England, 60 Pitcairn Road, Mitcham, Surrey CR4 4LL. Tel: 01-640 5431

The Forum on the Rights of Elderly People to Education (FREE) c/o Age Concern England.

Help the Aged, Education Department, St James' Walk, London EC1R OBE. Tel: 01-253 0253

The National Institute of Adult Continuing Education, 19b de Montfort Street, Leicester LE1 7GE. Tel: 0533-551451
Many publications on Adult Education including twice-yearly catalogues of short residential courses.

National Extension College, 18 Brooklands Avenue, Cambridge CB2 1PD.
A wide variety of correspondence courses

Open University, PO Box 71, Milton Keynes MK7 6AG.
As well as long term courses, the OU offers many short courses and packages suitable for individual or group study.

The following can provide addresses for local contacts:
National Adult School Organisation, Norfolk House, Smallbrook, Queensway, Birmingham B5 4LJ. Tel: 021-643 9297
Nationwide network of informal study groups

Pensioners Link (*Greater London Only*), 17 Balfe Street, London N1 9EB. Tel: 01–278 5501

Community Service Volunteers, 237 Pentonville Road, London N1 9NJ. Tel: 01–278 6601

University of the Third Age, 6 Parkside Gardens, London SW19 5EY. *9" × 4" s.a.e.*

College of Health, 18 Victoria Park Square, Bethnal Green, London E2 9PF.

Pensioners Voice (National Federation of Old Age Pensions Associations), 28 Bright St, Barton Hill, Bristol BS5 9PR. *Campaigning for pensioners' rights.*

Local Libraries and Town Halls or Education Departments will supply lists of activities, addresses of branches of WEA, Age Concern, Adult Education classes, Adult Basic Literacy and Numeracy tutors, Community and Leisure Centres, Citizens' Advice Bureau and Volunteer Bureau.

3   Health in Later Years

College of Health, 18 Victoria Park Square, London E2 9PF.

Royal National Institute for the Blind, 226 Great Portland Street, London W1N 6AA.

British Deaf Association, 38 Victoria Place, Carlisle CA1 1EX.

British Association for the Hard of Hearing, 16 Park Street, Windsor, Berks SL4 1LU.

Council for the Professions Supplementary to Medicine, York House, Westminster Bridge Road, London SE1.

United Kingdom Central Council for Nursing, Midwifery and Health Visiting (UKCC), 23 Portland Place, London W1.

4   Income in Retirement

HM Inspector of Anatomy, DHSS, Eileen House, 80–94 Newington Causeway, London SE1.

British Insurance Brokers Association (BIBA), 130 Fenchurch Street, London EC3.

Court of Protection, 25 Store Street, London WC1.

CRUSE, the Association of Widows, 126 Sheen Road, Richmond, Surrey.

Disabled Living Foundation, 380 Harrow Road, London W9 2HU.

Employment Fellowship, Drayton House, Gordon Street, London WC1.

National Association of Funeral Directors, 57 Doughty Street, London WC1.

Life Offices Association, Aldermary House, Queen Street, London EC4.

The London Stock Exchange, London EC2.

Motability, 14 Carlton Gardens, London SW1.

National Association of Security Dealers and Investment Managers (NASDIM), 25 Lovat Lane, London EC3.

Pre-Retirement Association, 19 Undine Street, London SW17.

Private Patients Plan, Eynsham House, Crescent Road, Tunbridge Wells, Kent.

RADAR, 25 Mortimer Street, London W1.

REACH (the Retired Executives Clearing House), Victoria House, Southampton Row, London WC1.

SAGA Holidays, PO Box 60, Folkestone, Kent.

Success after 60, 40/41 Old Bond Street, London W1.

5   House and Home

Counsel and Care for the Elderly, 131 Middlesex Street, London E1. Tel: 01-621 1624

General advice and information on accommodation and grants to individuals considered for residential care or home nursing services.

Disabled Living Foundation, (for address see above).

Information on aids for the disabled.

Elderly Accommodation Counsel Ltd., 182/184 Campden Hill Road, London W8. Tel: 01-243 8545.

A national computer database listing of all types of accommodation for elderly people.

Equipment for the Disabled, Mary Marlborough Lodge, Nuffield Orthopaedic Centre, Headington, Oxford OX3 7LD.

Friends of the Earth, 377 City Road, London EC1B 1NA.
Both for advice on heating and insulation.

House Builders Federation, 82 New Cavendish Square, London W1N 8AD.
List of private developers offering sheltered housing.

National House-Building Council, 58 Portland Place, London W1N 4BU.

National Mobility Office (for tenants), County Hall, Westminster Bridge Road, London SE1 7PB.

Neighbourhood Energy Action Information Centre, 2–4 Bigg Market, Newcastle-upon-Tyne NE1 1UW.

Royal Institute of British Architects, 66 Portland Place, London W1N 4AB.

Royal Institute of Chartered Surveyors, 12 Great George Street, Parliament Square, London SW1P 3AD.

Tenants Exchange Scheme, PO Box 170, London SW1 3PX.

7   Coping with Death and Bereavement

Practical Help
Wills

Citizens' Advice Bureaux (telephone directory or public library will give address of local branch) will advise on the making of wills and financial matters and will refer to a solicitor or a Legal Advice Centre if this seems appropriate.

Age Concern have forms which can be completed giving instructions as to the whereabouts of various documents and information about affairs to help next of kin, but these are not substitute wills which must be properly drawn up and witnessed.

Funeral arrangements

For those who want to make arrangements for their body:

1   To bequeath your body write to Professor of Anatomy at your nearest medical school or direct to HM Inspector of Anatomy, Department of Health and Social Services, Alexander Fleming House, Elephant and Castle, London SE1 6BY (01-703 6380).

2   To donate your organs for transplant: Multi-donor cards are now available. If you wish to donate any organ for transplant, complete a card and carry it with you. Cards are available at hospitals, chemists' shops, doctors' surgeries, Citizens' Advice Bureaux and post offices.

When someone dies who carries a card, phone the number on the card *immediately*.

When someone dies you will need to contact:

1   Registrar of Births and Deaths. Deaths have to be registered in the local registry office covering the area in which the death occurred. A list of the addresses and telephone numbers of local registry offices is usually displayed in post offices, public libraries, other public buildings and doctors' surgeries.

2   To apply for the death grant: forms are available from local social security offices and can be applied for on the back of a death certificate. The death certificate or other evidence of death must accompany the application, together with the deceased's marriage certificate, if married, and any national insurance contribution card and Department of Health and Social Services payment books you may still have. The grant varies from £9 to £30 depending on the age of the person who has died.

To arrange a funeral:

Most funeral directors are members of the National Association of Funeral Directors, 57 Doughty Street, London WC1

(01-242 9388) and must conform to a code of practice which includes the production of written estimates. If this is acceptable they can make all the necessary arrangements for the funeral service, although those with a religious faith will want to contact their parish clergy direct.

For those who die with insufficient funds to pay the funeral expenses, application can be made for supplementary benefit through the Department of Health and Social Services. If there is no one to make arrangements and the person dies in hospital, the hospital administrator will arrange the funeral. If the person dies in the community, the Director of Social Services has a responsibility to make these arrangements.

Age Concern England has recently been discussing the development of Funeral Planning Societies which could make it easier for families to discuss these arrangements when they are fit and healthy, and so reduce the pressure and anxiety on bereaved relatives who feel that they must arrange an elaborate funeral, incurring more expenses than the deceased would have wished them to do.

For advice and counselling in bereavement
National organisations
CRUSE (see p. 163 for address) – for widows, widowers and other members of the family.

Age Concern England (see p. 161 for address) – for the elderly bereaved.

Samaritans – For those in despair or tempted to suicide; phone at any time of the day or night. Telephone number is in the local telephone directory. General office is Slough 32713.

London Bereavements Projects Group, c/o London Voluntary Services Council, 68 Charlton Street, London NW1 1JR – who keep a list of the addresses of bereavement counselling groups.

FURTHER READING

2   Adding Spice to Life: Leisure

A useful bibliography on Education and Elderly People, prepared jointly with FREE, is published by The Centre for Policy on Ageing, Nuffield Lodge Studio, Regent's Park, London NW1 4RS.

4   Income in Retirement

Your Taxes and Savings, published by Age Concern England.
Easy Cooking for One or Two by Louise Davies, Penguin Books, 1972.

5   House and Home

General housing advice

Age Concern housing fact sheets: *Raising an income from your home*; *Improving and repairing your own home*; *Accommodation for the elderly*; *Help with heating*; *Advice on housing associations*, and others.
Available from Age Concern England (address on p. 161). Please send s.a.e.
Your Housing in Retirement by Janet Casey. Available also from Age Concern England – as above.
   This is the best source of practical advice on all aspects of housing with lots of useful addresses.
Moving Home in Retirement? by Lorna Gordon and Rose Moreno. Available from: SHAC, 189 Old Brompton Road, London SW5.
Heating Help in Retirement by Energy Inform Ltd. Available from Age Concern England – as above.

For tenants

Your Right to Repairs by SHAC. Available from SHAC (address as above).

For owner occupiers

Staying Put: Help for older Home Owners by Michael Corp and John Campbell of Anchor Housing Trust. Available from Age Concern England.

Buying or adapting a house or flat: a consumer guide for disabled people, by Sarah Langton-Lockton and Rosalind Purcell. Available from: Centre on Environment for the Handicapped, 126 Albert Street, London NW1 7NF.

For a list of 'Staying Put', 'Care and Repair' or similar schemes to help organise repairs or improvements, write, enclosing s.a.e., to Age Concern England (address p. 161).

6 Residential Care

HOLMES, T. H. and MASUDA, M. 'Life Change and Illness Susceptibility,' *Separation and Depression,* AAAS USA, 1973.

BREARLEY, P. *Admission to Residential Care,* Tavistock Publications, 1980.

Home for Life, a code of practice for residential care. Published by The Centre for Policy on Ageing (address p. 167).

7 Coping with Death and Bereavement

BOWLBY, J. *Attachment and Loss,* Vol 1: Attachment, Hogarth Press, 1969. Penguin Books, 1971.

BREARLEY, C. P. *Social Work, Ageing and Society,* Routledge & Kegan Paul, 1975.

GAINE, Michael. 'Ageing and the Spirit' in *The Social Challenge of Ageing,* edited by David Hobman, Croom Helm, 1978.

KÜBLER-ROSS, E. *On Death and Dying,* Tavistock Publications, 1973.

LEARED, Jean. 'Bereavement and Mourning', *Social Work Today,* Vol 9, no 45, 1978.

PARKES, C. M. *Bereavement – Studies of Grief in Adult Life,* Penguin Books, 1975.

—— 'Components of the Reaction to Loss of a Limb, Spouse or Home' in *Journal of Psychosomatic Research*, Vol 16, pp. 342–349.

—— *Facing Death*, National Extension College, Cambridge, 1981.

PINCUS, L. *The Challenge of a Long Life*, Faber & Faber, 1981.

SCHWARZMANN, B. 'Observations on the Dynamics at Play in a Group of Older People' in *Medical Social Work*, Vol 19, no 5, September 1966.

STERN, Karl, WILLIAMS, G. M., and PRADOS, M. 'Grief Reactions in Later Life' in *American Journal of Psychiatry*, Vol 108, 1951.

STOTT, M. *Ageing for Beginners*, Basil Blackwell, Oxford, 1981.

WILLANS, J. H. *Death and Bereavement*. Age Concern, Manifesto Series No 17, 1974 – Specialist Report, Age Concern, National Old People's Welfare Council.

Useful Publications
What to Do after a Death, DHSS.
What to Do when Someone Dies, The Consumers' Association, 14 Buckingham Street, London WC2N 6DS.
Wills and Probate, The Consumers' Association.
Write Your Own Will by Keith Best, Elliot Right Way Books, 1978.
What Happens when Someone Dies: Income Tax and Capital Gains Tax, Inland Revenue.

REFERENCES

1 Changing Relationships

DE BEAUVOIR, Simone. *Old Age*, Andre Deutsch; Weidenfeld & Nicolson, 1972.

COMFORT, Alex. *A Good Age*, Mitchell Beazley, 1977.

2   Adding Spice to Life: Leisure

JONES, Sidney. 'The Educational Experience in Homes and Hospitals' in *Outreach Education and the Elders: Theory and Practice*, edited by F. Glendenning, Beth Johnson Foundation, 1980.

FERNAU, C. in *Labour Education* No 53, 1983–4.

6   Old People – New Lives: Residential Care

1. RIGHTON, P. 'Positive and Negative Aspects of Residential Care', *Social Work Today*, Vol 8, no 37, 1977.

2. CLOUGH, R. *Old Age Homes*, George Allen & Unwin, 1981.

3. CLOUGH, R. and WIGG, M. 'The Workhouse Re-visited', *Social Work Today*, Vol 13, no 24, 1982.

4. McDERMENT, Li and GREENGROSS, S. *International Trends in Residential Provision for the Elderly*, Social Care Association. To be published 1985.

5. HMSO. *Growing Older*, Cmnd 8173. (London HMSO), 1981.

6. Ibid.

7. Ibid.

8. Ibid.

9. AMANN, A. 'The Status and Prospects of the Ageing in Western Europe', *Eurosocial*, occasional papers no 8, 1981.

10. HMSO. *Growing Older*, Cmnd 8173. (London HMSO), 1981.

11. AMANN, A. op cit.

12. BLOOM, L. Z., COBURN, K. and PEARLMAN, J. *The New Assertive Woman*, New York, Delacorte Press, 1975.

13. MORONEY, R. M. *The Family and the State*, Longman, 1976.

14. DHSS. 'Some Aspects of Residential Care', *Social Work Service* 10 (July), 3–17, 1976.

15. McDERMENT, Li and GREENGROSS, S. op cit.
16. Ibid.
17. HARRIS, A. I. *Social Welfare for the Elderly*, Government Social Survey, HMSO, 1968.
18. BREARLEY, C. P. *Residential Work with the Elderly*, p. 28, Routledge & Kegan Paul, 1977.
19. Ibid, p. 28.

7 Coping with Death and Bereavement

1. BUTLER, Robert. 'Just Old Age?' in *Social Work Today*, Vol 9, No 47, 8.8.78.
2. PARKES, C. Murray. Introduction to *On Death and Dying* by E. Kübler-Ross, Tavistock Publications, 1973.
3. WILLANS, Joan H. *Death and Bereavement*, Age Concern, Manifesto Series No 17, 1974.
4. STOTT, Mary. *Ageing for Beginners*, Basil Blackwell, Oxford, 1981.
5. HOBMAN, David. 'Encountering Death in Old Age' in *Social Work Today*, Vol 10 No 2, 5.9.78.
6. St. John's Gospel, 14:1.

Index